PERRY GROVES' FOOTBALL HEROES

Twenty of the Greatest Goal-scorers, Hardest Tacklers and Biggest Rogues Ever to Grace the Game

PERRY GROVES

with John McShane

JOHN BLAKE

To Lewis and Drew: Keep on making me proud and
striving to achieve.
To George and Alf: Make the most of your talents.
And to my gorgeous Jose, beautiful on the inside and out:
Much love.

Published by John Blake Publishing Ltd,
3 Bramber Court, 2 Bramber Road,
London W14 9PB, England

www.johnblakepublishing.co.uk

First published in hardback in 2009

ISBN: 978-1-84454-608-4

British Library Cataloguing-in-Publication Data:

A catalogue record for this book is available from the British Library.

Design by www.envydesign.co.uk

Printed in the UK by CPI William Clowes Beccles NR34 7TL

1 3 5 7 9 10 8 6 4 2

Papers used by John Blake Publishing are natural, recyclable
products made from wood grown in sustainable forests.
The manufacturing processes conform to the environmental
regulations of the country of origin.

Photographs © Action Images, Cleva Media, Getty and Rex Features

CONTENTS

PROLOGUE

A little while back, I wrote a book called *We All Live in a Perry Groves World*. It put into black and white what a lot of people who knew me or had seen me play had known for years – I was a cult. Yes, that's right, cult! And with the publication of the book it became official.

For some reason, fans remembered my efforts on the field, sang songs about me and had devoted websites to my life. So my book told of my growing up as a football-mad kid in East Anglia and how I started out as a teenager at Colchester United, was George Graham's first signing at Arsenal, won two championship medals with the Gooners and then went to Southampton, only to have my career ended at 28 by injury.

I also mentioned how I probably drank too much and played around with the ladies too often, and what I and other players got up to off the field. I also recalled what a great time it all was and how I enjoyed every minute of it.

To the surprise of many people, not least yours truly, the book was a great success. Yet, although it touched on some of my early influences, I didn't go into detail about those men I'd worshipped as a kid or came to play with or against later on. Nor did I mention the players I've admired since I quit the game. Now I'm putting that right.

The simple reason is that anyone who has ever kicked a football has heroes. They may be some of the most famous players ever to walk on to a pitch, men whose every move is watched by countless millions in this television age and whose image is instantly recognisable. Or they could be forgotten foot soldiers who played in front of empty terraces yet bring back memories from a long-lost youth. It doesn't matter. Either way, they are imprinted on your mind and are with you forever. And, most importantly, they make you smile at the very thought of them.

Everyone has a list of their own football heroes and it won't tally with mine. Why should it? We all look for a different quality in the players we love to watch.

Some of the legends – Pele, Cruyff, Beckenbauer, Moore – would make the hit parade of virtually every football fan. But Anders Limpar, Kevin Beattie, Teofilo Cubillas? That's a different matter. And as for Terry Hurlock!

Let me explain. This is not the list of the Greatest Footballers Who've Ever Lived, although they are all pretty good, I hasten to add. Nor is it a reference book with microscopic detail of their careers. These are just the

20 I reckon had that something that you can't put into words. You could call it star quality, charisma, presence, whatever. Some of them went on to great things when their playing careers ended and became part of world football's hierarchy. Others went broke, became alcoholics or even tried to commit suicide. That's the way it goes.

I've tried to keep it light-hearted though, because I think football is meant to be enjoyed and it's the memories of our heroes' achievements on the field that we all cherish. They range from images I remember as a little kid glued to the TV in our front room in Suffolk years ago to modern stars I see week in week out, either live or on television. And by some curious coincidence a lot of the men I admired on the field seemed to be even more active off it when it came to wine, women and song.

I was lucky enough to meet or play with or against many of the men on my list. Bobby Moore gave me advice on drinking. Terry Hurlock got me involved in a mass brawl in a pub. David Seaman told me why he liked to spend all night sleeping on riverbanks and Kevin Beattie suffered one of the strangest injuries I ever came across in football – a terrible mishap in a dressing-room toilet minutes before kick-off.

If there are some players I've missed out, I'm sorry, but I can't write about everybody. I just hope reading about my heroes, mates and memories gives you half the pleasure they have given me. And if you don't agree with my choices then there's a simple answer – do your own book.

CHAPTER 1

BOBBY MOORE

The best piece of advice I ever heard from a footballer came from Bobby Moore, one of the greatest players ever. He was a living legend who will always be remembered as captain of the World Cup-winning side of 1966: handsome, clean-cut, immaculate, the first golden boy of English football.

I had just left Colchester United for Arsenal and I was in awe of him. Everything he said is still lodged in my memory all these years later. And what were those words from a man with an encyclopaedic knowledge of football and of life? He said, 'Never refuse a drink, because there'll come a day when nobody wants to buy you one.'

And there was more. 'Make sure you drink in halves, not pints. If you're seen knocking back pints, people think you're pissed. If it's halves, they think you're a professional.' How very profound. I've never forgotten those words.

I never tire of telling this story because it shows that he wasn't just a great player, he was a proper geezer too. Everybody said that Bobby Moore had no pace. He couldn't head the ball either. Come to think of it, his left foot was nothing to talk about. Apart from that, he had everything.

Geoff Hurst, who knew him better than most, observed, 'People said that he wasn't particularly good in the air, but nobody outran him and nobody outjumped him. He was able to read the game at the back like nobody else.'

If you look at a picture of Bobby Moore as England captain handing over a pennant to his rival skipper before kick-off and then one of him walking off 90 minutes later, he looked exactly the same. It was as if he hadn't been in a game. His barnet was never ruffled, he didn't seem to attract mud to his body or kit, and heaven forbid that he had broken into a sweat at any stage.

After climbing the Wembley stairs to collect the World Cup trophy from the Queen after two hours in the boiling sun playing the Germans, he even found time to pause and wipe his hands on his shorts and the velvet draping in the Royal Box before collecting his medal. He obviously didn't want to have sticky palms when he shook her hand – class – but the big surprise was that he must actually have been sweating at some point during that hot July afternoon.

Minutes later, he was hoisted aloft on the shoulders of Geoff Hurst and Ray Wilson and, with the trophy firmly in his grip, his picture was taken in an image that is as instantly recognisable today as it was in the week of that victory. That image – up there on his mates' shoulders in a moment of victory – should have been the one that most people remember of Bobby Moore, but four years later there was an even more memorable photograph that captured the essence of the man.

This time it was after a defeat, the 1–0 loss to Brazil in the Mexico World Cup, a game that everyone who saw it still regards as one of the finest ever.

I was just a toddler and the big thing about the tournament wasn't just that it gave us the Brazilian side of 1970 – often named as the best team ever – but also that it was being televised in colour. To this day I can remember how exciting it was to watch. And after that match Bobby Moore stripped to the waist and shook hands with Pele as they swapped shirts.

Moore looked like a Scandinavian film star, and Pele was as black as mahogany. The smiles of respect for each other on their faces as they shook hands is one of the enduring images of sport. I don't think Pele's English was very good at that time and I'm pretty sure that Bobby Moore's Portuguese wasn't all that hot, but it was as if there was an international language between them: 'You're a great player' and 'You're a great player too.'

It was during this game that Bobby Moore made a tackle that seems to get more famous as the years pass. It even got a mention in the lyrics of 'Three Lions', the 'football's coming home' song. One of the finest players in that Brazilian team was their right-winger Jairzinho, who went on to become one of the few players to score in every round of a World Cup finals. He'd already given his side the lead and England were pressing for an equaliser and had loads of bodies in the Brazil half. The temperature was in the high 80s (30C) and when an England attack broke down we had hardly anyone in defence as the Brazilians broke away.

Jairzinho raced in from the right, carrying the ball for a good 30 yards at pace, and I mean real pace, with the ball stuck to his right foot. Somehow or other Bobby Moore managed to track back with him, between the Brazilian and the goal, giving way as the Brazilian ran forward and deep into the area. Then at the last possible moment, when most other defenders would probably have been happy just to give a penalty away, he put out his right leg, the 'wrong' one for a tackle like that, and, using the outside of his foot, took it off the Brazilian with a combination of strength and nonchalance.

Jairzinho, legitimately robbed of the ball and his own momentum, tumbled to the ground while Moore calmly pushed the ball forward a couple of yards and gently played it clear along the ground to the feet of another England player. I don't know what it says about the English character, but almost four decades on that tackle is remembered more vividly and fondly than most goals the national side have scored since.

And it was that tackle that captured what was truly great about Bobby Moore. It was his reading of situations and his timing of tackles. If you tried to coach the way he played, you couldn't do it. Eight times out of ten he'd tackle with his 'wrong' foot or he'd use the outside of his foot – like that Jairzinho tackle – to win the ball. You would have thought he'd get injured that way, that his knees and ankles should have been vulnerable, but it never happened.

As tense and as gripping as the entire match was, it seems that Mooro didn't lose his sense of humour during it. One of the highlights is THAT save by Gordon Banks from Pele's header. It was hard and downwards, and bounced badly just inside the far post, but Banks, at full stretch, not only managed to get to it but also to flick the ball over the bar. It's generally reckoned to be the save of all time. Banks was laughing as he stood up afterwards but not out of delight at what he'd done. It was because Moore had said to him, 'You're getting old, Banksy. You used to hold on to them.'

Moore had a brilliant World Cup in Mexico. He stood head and shoulders above every other defender in the tournament. The only man to rival him, and perhaps his closest rival in 'the best defender ever' category, was Franz Beckenbauer of Germany. Moore's performance was all the more remarkable because he'd hardly had the smoothest run-up to the tournament. On the way to Mexico, England had been to the Colombian capital of Bogota and he'd been arrested for stealing a bracelet – a charge, incidentally, of which he was later totally cleared. Not much of a stitch-up job then!

Poor Bobby ended up under house arrest in the British Embassy, no doubt feeling a bit sorry for himself. Jimmy Greaves, one of the greatest goalscorers in English football history, happened to be in that neck of the woods at the time while taking part in a car rally. Greaves's international career was over by then but he was one of Bobby Moore's oldest mates in the game, so he decided to pop in and see him, even though he was not allowed visitors. Greavsie just climbed over a wall into a courtyard, got into the building and simply walked around the place until he found an unshaven Moore. Greaves later said it was the only time in his life that he ever saw Moore looking dishevelled. Just then a member of the embassy staff appeared and Greaves just said to him, ''Ere, mate, can you get us a couple of lagers?'

As well as being two of the most famous players in England's history, Moore and Greaves could drink for England too. And Scotland, Wales and Ireland, come to think of it. Greaves publicly admitted his drink problems in later years but Bobby managed to keep most of his boozing quiet. He even featured in a television advertising campaign for boozers called 'Pop into your local' when he and Martin Peters, both suited and booted, were seen taking their wives into a pub and playing darts with the locals.

One of the few times his liking for a sherbet came out in the open was when he went out with Greaves and West Ham team-mates Brian Dear and Clyde Best for a few drinks one New Year's Eve. It was at a nightclub in Blackpool owned by a mate of his, the boxer Brian London. They didn't go crazy and were back at their hotel by 1am(ish). Nothing wrong with that, apart from the fact that next day West Ham were hammered 4–0 in the Cup by Blackpool.

It was well known in football circles that Moore liked a drink and that after a game he would go out and get pissed, only ever downing halves of course, so people wouldn't think he was drinking much, but that's what they did in those days. You would see him and Greavsie out somewhere having Sunday lunch and a few bevvies in the same pubs where the fans would drink.

Like most schoolboys, I thought he was some sort of footballing god – he practically had a halo over his head. He had those Aryan looks – in an English way, that is – and he never got flustered.

Although he played for other sides, Bobby Moore will always be associated with West Ham. He was born in the heart of Hammers' land (Barking in Essex), grew up there, played his football there and is still revered so much that the number six shirt he wore for all those years was recently withdrawn by the club so no one else would wear it.

Moore joined the club as a schoolboy, coming under the guidance of one of the senior pros who happened to be their number six at the time, a certain Malcolm Allison who went on to coach Manchester City's finest hours. Moore made his debut at home in a 3–2 win against Manchester United in September 1958 and over the next 16 years played 544 games for West Ham. He captained them to the FA Cup victory over Preston North End (3–2) in 1964 and the following year picked up the European Cup Winners' Cup, again at Wembley, when the Hammers beat 1860 Munich 2–0.

But it was his England career that made him a legend.

He was included in the England Under-23 squad in 1960 at the age of 19, and his form for West Ham meant he was a last-minute addition to the senior squad that manager Walter Winterbottom took to Chile for the 1962 World Cup. His full England debut came on 20 May 1962 in the final warm-up game, a 4–0 win over Peru in Lima, and he was so impressive he kept his place for England throughout the tournament.

It's funny to think about where Bobby Moore made his first appearances on the world scene. Tournaments now come no bigger than the World Cup, yet back in 1962 in provincial Chile, none of the games in England's qualifying group attracted a crowd of even 10,000 to the Braden Copper Stadium in Rancagua, where all the games in the group were played.

In the 1958 World Cup, England had been criticised for choosing a large Stockholm hotel as their headquarters, so Winterbottom had accepted an invitation from the American-owned Braden Copper Company to pitch camp at Coya, a small settlement 2,500ft up in the Andes and an hour's drive from Rancagua. The players lived two to a bungalow and had their meals cooked by an Englishwoman. Boredom was a big problem and so were the tortuous trips down the mountain to play games. Johnny Haynes of Fulham, one of the England stars at the time, remembers the entire thing as 'crap'.

Jimmy Greaves remembers it in much the same way. He once said in an interview, 'The Braden bleeding Copper Company in a place called Rancagua. It was a factory with a sports pavilion and that was where we stayed. It was a cement and wood structure with a corrugated iron roof partitioned off into separate rooms. There, me and Bobby Moore would lie in our camp beds staring at that roof as the rain bounced off it. As for a mini-bar, all we wanted was a mini to find a bleeding bar, the nearest being in a golf club two miles away. We ate with the workers in the canteen and relaxed by staring into space. Come the big tournament itself, we played in front of between 2,000 and 5,000 people in a stadium which nowadays would just have been passed as a training ground. There were no England fans to be seen and the locals who were interested arrived on horseback.'

England lost the first game to Hungary 2–1, beat Argentina 3–1 in their second and got the point they needed in their third game in a goalless draw with Bulgaria – in front of 5,700 people. Having reached the quarter-final, England lost 3 1 to Brazil, who eventually won the tournament. Their right-winger Garrincha did most of the damage and scored two goals, but at least there was a decent crowd for this game at Vina del Mar – 17,736.

Greaves even remembers the defeat by Brazil in an unusual way: 'Thank goodness we finished second in our group and moved to a Valparaiso hotel – but even then Chile and the "glamour" of the World Cup was still something I was coming to terms with. It was awful. When Vava scored to make it 3–1 to Brazil in our quarter-final, it is the first time I have seen all the other 21 players go to congratulate him.'

No doubt Greavsie and Haynes are right – it might all have been 'crap' – but the big plus for England was the arrival of Bobby Moore. Even then criticisms about him were being aired: he was 'pedestrian, not up to much in the air, suspect stamina', according to some. He was playing more a traditional half-back role then, albeit a defensive one, rather than the central defender he was to become, but his class was already standing out.

In May 1963, on only his 12th appearance, he captained England for the first time, after Jimmy Armfield was ruled out by injury. At 22, he was the youngest player to do so. England won 4–2 and he got the job permanently the following year when new boss Alf Ramsey decided he was the man for him. Moore captained England 90 times, the same as Billy Wright, and ended up with 108 caps, breaking the record held by Bobby Charlton by just two appearances. Only Peter Shilton played more times for his country.

Those great days of 1966 and 1970 were never to be repeated. Moore was still at the heart of the defence when England failed to qualify for the 1974 finals but for once the man for whom the word 'immaculate' seemed to have been invented was at fault. He had won his 100th cap by then in a 5–0 trouncing of the Scots, but only Alan Ball and Martin Peters were left of the side of 1966 when England went to Poland and lost 2–0. Poor Bobby deflected the first past Peter Shilton and lost possession to gift them the second.

Ramsey decided to drop him for the vital second leg against Poland at Wembley that would see England eliminated. Moore asked Ramsey if that meant he wasn't required any more and was told: 'Of course not. I need you as my captain at the World Cup next year.'

But it wasn't to be. With England out of the World Cup, Ramsey was sacked a few months later. Bobby went on to win his last cap in the next game, a 1–0 defeat in a friendly with Italy on 14 November 1973.

His final appearance for the Hammers wasn't far away either. He was injured in an FA Cup tie against Hereford United in January 1974 and two months later he was transferred to Fulham for £25,000. The most famous Hammer of them all was gone.

His first game at Fulham was on 19 March against Middlesbrough at Craven Cottage, where the gate was doubled to 18,000 by his appearance. It wasn't a great start as Fulham lost 0–4, but they did defeat West Ham in a League Cup tie and reached the FA Cup Final in 1975 where they lost – to West Ham, of course – in his final Wembley appearance. He finally knocked it on the head after an away trip to Blackburn in May 1977, some 19 years after making his West Ham debut.

When football legends reached the end of the road in those days, there was always one last pit-stop they could make – America. It had happened before and it's certainly happened since. Bobby went on to play for two teams in the North American Soccer League: San Antonio Thunder, for whom he played 24 games in the summer of 1976, and then seven games for the Seattle Sounders. There was also an international swansong of sorts with appearances for 'Team USA' in games against the Italians, the Brazilians and an England team captained by Gerry Francis. Finally, there were a handful of games in 1978 for the Danish semi-professional club Herning Fremad.

Moore then tried his hand at managing. But – there's no polite way of putting this – he was pants as a manager. He wasn't alone in that when it came to the 1966 World Cup side: Nobby Stiles, Bobby Charlton and Alan Ball were all rubbish as far as I'm concerned. The only one who had any success was Jack Charlton, and that was at international level with Ireland rather than at club level with Middlesbrough. I think a lot of it is to do with the fact that they were outstanding players during their career. But, when it comes to managing and especially coaching, a lot of it is basic and former top players just can't understand why guys can't do what came naturally to them when they were younger.

Players weren't so much coached then as trained. They would be prepared for physical exertion rather than the tactics of the game with sprints and five-a-side and so on. Even under Alf Ramsey it would just be what formation to adopt and then training to keep fit. They were such good players that they made their own decisions on the field. Lesser players have to be told what to do over and over again but the top players, if they have to be told at all, only need to be told once and it sinks in.

Moore was in charge at Southend when I was at Colchester. I knew some of the lads down there and when they did something wrong or were in the wrong position he would have a job to understand why they did it. To the great players, these things came instinctively. In fairness to Bobby, though, I know from the lads at Southend that he never looked down his nose at any of them or gave them the feeling he was superior. He wasn't that kind of guy.

Sometimes when a side is winning easily their fans chant, 'Can we play you every week?' at the opposition. That was how I felt about Southend during the time Bobby was there. I managed to score nine goals against them in a calendar year: two hat-tricks, one brace and a single goal in the other game. The match where I got a couple ended up with us winning 5–2 away; Moore passed me in the corridor after the match and said, 'Well played, son.' I was overwhelmed. To begin with, he had recognised me! And, second, for one of the all-time legends of football to say, 'Well played' made me feel about 12ft tall.

Some people outside football might think it strange that he would say that to me after I'd just helped hammer a couple of nails into his coffin. But football doesn't work like that and, more to the point, he wasn't that sort of bloke. I'm not saying my goals against his side helped to get him sacked, but it wouldn't have done him any favours. Southend were our local rivals and their players were probably on two or three times what we were earning at the time.

My mate Roy McDonough, who'd been at Colchester with me, was at Southend during the time Bobby was there. He would always say that Bobby Moore was a man's man. He didn't mind you going out and having a sherbet or socialising. His ethos was that, if you work hard and play hard, you have to make sure you perform. A lot of players at the lower level go out and get pissed and then their performances on the pitch don't justify them being the boy-about-town. Roy could drink for England but his performances at that level were still excellent. I think that's why he and Bobby got on so well, because he was from an era when they all drank, didn't they?

The next time I met Bobby was at Colchester for a testimonial for Micky Cook, who played something like 10,000 games for the club. I was at Arsenal by this time and Micky asked me to come back and guest for him. It was Colchester against an International XI or a West Ham XI, that sort of opposition. George Graham refused permission for me to play because of insurance problems, but I went anyway.

I played for a bit for the Colchester side and Bobby Moore was a guest player too. As it was a testimonial, I came off after 20 minutes and went into the dressing room – it was more like a cupboard at Colchester – and had my shower. When I came out, there was Bobby, who had obviously come off at about the same time. So there we were, just the two of us in the changing rooms: me fresh out of the shower and the bloke in the corner taking his boots off, Bobby Moore. For once in my life I didn't know what to say.

He broke the ice. He just looked up and said, 'All right, Grovesy? It's going all right, isn't it?' He obviously meant that he'd seen I'd gone from Colchester to Arsenal and got in the first team. I was like that character Perry in the Harry Enfield show who says, 'Yes, Mrs Patterson. No, Mrs Patterson' and 'Thank you, Mrs Patterson' whenever his friend Kevin's parents talk to him. All I could think of saying was 'Yes, thanks.'

Without being patronising or condescending, he said,

'All you need to do is enjoy yourself and believe in yourself.' Then he said, 'I know you will do all right.'

Rightly or wrongly, I took that to mean that he had seen me play, knew what I could do, and that I would be all right at that level. So I just said, 'Yep, that's what I'm doing.'

I hadn't been a Gooner very long, perhaps half a season, and, number one, he knew who I was. Number two, he was talking to me. Number three, he was saying, whether he believed it or not, that I had talent. I thought I'd better say something back, so, as he'd come off early, I said, 'Are you struggling?'

'No, son,' he replied. 'Too old, too old.' Then he said, 'George is a hard taskmaster, isn't he?'

'The training's not too hard,' I said, because I'd been used to harder at Colchester, 'but it is more intense.'

'Just listen,' he said, 'and you won't go far wrong.' He then headed for the showers. I thanked him and he said, 'Good luck, son.'

I never did get round to showing him the high spots of Colchester that night! Come to think of it, if that meeting had happened 20 years later I'd have asked him if he still had that shirt he swapped with Pele: I could have sold it on eBay.

Eventually, he got the sack from Southend and I think it's a disgrace the way the football establishment treated him after that. If he had been German, he would have become an ambassador for the sport like Franz Beckenbauer. If he'd been French, he could have ended up with the prestige of someone like Michel Platini. Over here, it was, 'Oh yeah, Bobby Moore. He was our captain when we won the World Cup. See ya.'

He did some radio work later in life but it's only when someone like him dies that people wring their hands and start paying the tributes they didn't bother to make during his life. Now there's a stand at West Ham named after him and there are statues in his honour at Upton Park and Wembley.

He was only 51 when he died from bowel cancer. It also emerged that he'd had testicular cancer as early as 1962 but he'd kept it quiet because of the shadow surrounding the illness then and the effects it might have had on his career. He'd been awarded an OBE in 1967 but he never got the knighthood that other footballers did. Bobby Charlton and Geoff Hurst both ended up as 'Sir' and good luck to them, but if ever any player deserved a knighthood it was 'Sir' Bobby Moore.

CHAPTER 2

KEVIN BEATTIE

I wouldn't want anyone thinking that I had no mates as a kid and that I just sat in front of the television with my Pot Noodles waiting for the football to come on. That said, the first time I remember watching Kevin Beattie was on television. Not on *Match of the Day*, which I watched religiously every Saturday night, but on *Match of the Week*.

I was living near Colchester at the time and that was the name of ITV's Sunday-afternoon football magazine programme in our area. Unlike the BBC programme, it was regionalised, so that in London – where it was called *The Big Match* – you would have Arsenal, Spurs, QPR etc, while in the Midlands it would be Aston Villa, West Brom, Wolves, Coventry and so on. The three big teams in our area – Anglia TV – were Ipswich, Norwich and Luton, who were all in the top flight around that time, although once a season you'd have Colchester, Peterborough, Northampton and Southend highlights as well.

The commentator on the games in our area would always be the legendary Gerry Harrison. He'd say, 'The full-back has passed it to number six, number six passes it to the centre-forward, the centre-forward passes it to the left-winger who crosses and the number nine scores!' Perhaps I'm being a little harsh on Gerry, but you get the drift. It was the days of kipper ties and sheepskin jackets for commentators and managers off the pitch, and home-perms and shoulder-length barnets on it. The fashions might look a nightmare now, but it was great to settle down in front of the box on a Sunday after I'd played for my team Cornard Dynamos in the morning and come home for my bath and then Sunday dinner.

At that time, Ipswich were managed by Bobby Robson. He was a great manager and, of course, ended up as Sir Bobby after being in charge of England and a host of big clubs at home and abroad. He used to annoy local coaches around Suffolk and Norfolk, though, because he'd bring down coach-loads of kids from his native North East for trials and the local teams thought it meant their youngsters would end up being overlooked.

Ipswich striker Eric Gates, who won a couple of England caps, was from Sir Bobby's neck of the woods but the best of them all was Kevin Beattie. You can't blame Robson for trawling the North if you unearth a 'diamond' – which is what Sir Bobby often called him – like Kevin. Robson would even go on to say that he was the best English-born player he had ever seen and this was from a man who'd played with or managed the likes of Duncan Edwards, Bobby Charlton and Gazza. At one stage Kevin was called 'the new Bobby Moore', but he was most frequently likened to Edwards – the powerful young Manchester United star who died in the Munich air crash.

Kevin was actually from Carlisle and there is a wonderful story about how he came to sign for Ipswich. He'd been watched by Liverpool and had gone there for a trial. He got off the train at Lime Street Station alone, a nervous teenager carrying his boots wrapped in paper. There was no one from Anfield to meet him so he sat around for an hour and then assumed they'd lost interest. So he got back on a train and went home. In fact, the Liverpool official failed to meet the train by mistake and so they'd let a 15-year-old gem slip through their fingers.

Liverpool's legendary manager Bill Shankly said, 'If he hasn't got the brains to find his way from Lime Street to Anfield we don't want to sign him.' Big mistake, Shanks. But, in fairness to him, in later years he did take Kevin aside and say, 'I haven't made many mistakes, but you were one of the biggest.'

A week later, Kevin made it to Ipswich. He was wearing his father's shoes as he didn't have a proper pair of his own, and the football boots were still in a paper bag. This time, however, he was met by someone from the club. Sir Bobby had taken no chances. The youngster was escorted from Euston Station by Ipswich chief scout Ron Gray, who'd been bluntly told by the boss, 'If you miss him, you've lost your job.' The manager said that when Kevin did eventually arrive it was with 'a hole in his trousers and sixpence in his pocket'. A slight exaggeration perhaps, but not by much. He was given some shirts and ties by the club and the very next day played for the reserves against Fulham.

The highly respected Gray, who brought a host of players to Ipswich, immediately phoned Robson to say, 'This lad'll be in the first team at 19.' He got that wrong – Kevin made his debut at 18.

He actually arrived as a striker but Sir Bobby turned him into a defender and that changed his life completely. Kevin has gone on record as saying that, once he moved to the back of the team, the game was in front of him and it made it even easier. He didn't have to turn and look both ways like forwards do, and it became clear that's where his best position was, either in central defence or as left-back.

'What a player the boy was,' Robson said of him later. 'He could climb higher than the crossbar and still head the ball down. He had the sweetest left foot I've ever seen and could hit 60-yard passes, without looking, that eliminated six opposition players from the game. He had the strength of a tank, was lightning quick and he could tackle.' Again not the complete player, he had no big throw. 'I was so grateful he was on my side, because as a player I would have hated to play against him.'

Now, why didn't anyone ever describe me like that?

Kevin's first-team debut for Ipswich came in the opening game of the 1972/73 season and Ipswich won 2–1. That would be a good enough start, but the team they beat was a Manchester United side with Denis Law, Bobby Charlton and George Best in it. And the game was at Old Trafford. Afterwards, a teenage Kevin asked Bobby Charlton for his autograph. Signing it, Charlton said Kevin reminded him of Duncan Edwards and that Kevin would be the one signing autographs for many years to come.

This was a golden era for Ipswich. As well as 'The Beat' – which was what everyone in football called him – and Gates, they had Colin Viljoen, John Wark, Mick Mills and Trevor Whymark, and they were one of the best teams in the country.

It was only a few months after his first-team debut that he was capped for England Under-23s. Kevin went on to win nine England caps – Sir Bobby said it should have been 99 or more – but injuries were to play a big part in his life. His international career even survived the embarrassment of getting off a train heading for Scotland and a Hampden Park clash with their Under-23s when the train pulled into Carlisle. He saw the station nameplate, felt homesick and simply got off.

Kevin was a colossus on the pitch. He dominated in the air, he had a fantastic left foot and was pinging balls everywhere. That transformation into a defender was a masterstroke. Playing at centre-half or left-back, he looked like one of those players who had a horseshoe in his boot. He could hit the ball miles and his range of passing was fantastic. He had a ferocious shot on him too and he didn't mind shooting from 30 yards or more. And he was quick.

So that was the player I used to watch on *Match of the Week*. He was described at the time as a boy trapped in a man's body, but what did I know? There was always a guy in the Under-12s at any club who had a beard and hairy legs and turned up on a moped, and in his way this was The Beat. He seemed like a man-mountain. It's amazing how certain players have a presence and an aura about them. I was lucky enough to train and play with him at Colchester United at the end of his career and he was only 5ft 10in. He was no bigger than me and in my eyes that made him even more of a fantastic player. When he was playing, it seemed as though he was one of the biggest men on the pitch. He was a legend to me even then, although I wasn't going to tell him that, but it made him even more impressive in my eyes to know that he could somehow 'grow' into a giant once he stepped on a football field. You can't buy presence.

The Beat was the first great player I had been lucky enough to train with and I just wanted to see how good he was. They say you should never meet your heroes because you'll be disappointed, but he blew that one out of the water. When I met him and trained with him, he turned out to be the nicest man you could wish to meet – a top geezer.

When he came to Colchester – for a very brief period in the early 1980s – his knees were all shot due to the injuries and cortisone injections he'd had. Yet, even injured and into his thirties, he was still the quickest player at the club over ten yards by a long way. One of my great assets was pace and he was the only one who nearly beat me in a race. So I'm glad I never came up against him in his prime.

The years that had passed since his debut against Manchester United and those Sunday afternoons I'd seen him on the box hadn't been too kind to him. His career had started off superbly but injuries had stopped him from achieving the greatness everyone reckoned was his for the taking.

In his first season at Portman Road (1972/73), Ipswich won the Texaco Cup by beating Norwich City and finished fourth in the league, which meant they qualified for Europe. The following season they came fourth again and in the UEFA Cup beat Lazio, Twente Enschede of Holland and a little side called Real Madrid before going out in the quarter-finals. Ipswich also beat Manchester United at Old Trafford again, this time in the FA Cup, The Beat scoring the only goal of the match with a header. The year ended with him winning the inaugural Young Player of the Year award and all those hopes of everyone who rated him seemed about to be fulfilled.

The following year, Ipswich finished third in the league and were unlucky to lose to West Ham in a replayed FA Cup semi-final. It wasn't a question of *if* Kevin would play for the full England side but *when*, and in April 1975 he got his first cap. The game was a European Championship qualifier against Cyprus and is best remembered for Malcolm Macdonald scoring all five goals in the 5–0 victory. That was a good start for Kevin – he played in the centre of defence and had a goal disallowed for a foul on the goalkeeper.

He was also one of the stars of another memorable England performance soon after that, a 5–1 thrashing of Scotland at Wembley. It's one of those games that the Scots hate to be reminded of, so here goes. England's skipper was Alan Ball and alongside him were Colin Bell and Gerry Francis. Mick Channon tore the Scots apart with his direct running up front and they had no idea how to handle Kevin Keegan, frizzy barnet and all. But The Beat was as good as any of them. He played at left-back, although that didn't seem to mean all that much on that afternoon as he was everywhere.

England were already ahead through a goal after five minutes from Francis when Ball and Keegan combined down the right a couple of minutes later. When Keegan's cross came over, Channon was racing to get into the box to meet it, but somehow or other The Beat had got there first – and, remember, he was left-back. There was the little matter of two Scottish defenders to be sorted out but he outmuscled and outjumped them both and looped a great header into the top right-hand corner of the net. It was recently voted one of the top 50 goals ever scored for England. The Wild Man of Borneo had arrived.

Kevin would undoubtedly have been in the national side throughout the 1970s and beyond if accidents and those injuries hadn't taken their toll. In 1977, Ipswich were chasing the title and were well placed at Easter, only for Kevin to get badly burned in a bonfire at his home. He'd decided that the fire needed stoking up so he threw some petrol on it. Our Kev was never going to be a rocket scientist, was he? He was forced to miss six games

– Ipswich lost four of them and finished five points behind the eventual winners Liverpool. Bobby Robson reckoned that with The Beat in their side they'd have won the championship.

During these glory days, Kevin was a key member of the Ipswich side that beat Barcelona, Johan Cruyff and all, 3–0 in the UEFA Cup and in 1978 he was a member of the Ipswich team that beat Arsenal 1–0 in the Cup Final. On the way up the steps to collect his medal, he was offered a lit cigarette by an Ipswich fan. He smoked it, hid it as he shook the VIPs' hands and then took some more drags as he came down the steps. Throughout his career The Beat – whose eyesight was so bad he later said he couldn't see clearly what was going on but played a lot 'by intuition' – smoked 20 cigarettes a day.

There were lots of great days but the injuries were plaguing him. If anyone thinks it's all wonderful in the Glory Game, just look at what he said recently about that period: 'My knees were knackered. According to modern medical science, three cortisone injections in a lifetime is about enough, whereas I was having three every game, two before the kick-off and one at half-time. I certainly don't blame anyone, the injections were given in all good faith. Sadly, I think it has now been proved that, like thalidomide, at the time cortisone was unsafe and could have devastating side-effects.'

There's not one ounce of bitterness in his statement, but it shows that players are just a piece of meat – if you can't play, then you're no use to the manager or anyone.

He might have won a UEFA Cup winner's medal in

1981 but broke his arm in the FA Cup semi-final defeat against Manchester City, so he missed the two-leg European triumph over Dutch side AZ '67 Alkmaar. Twenty-seven years later, he was belatedly given a winner's medal by UEFA President Michel Platini who had been one of the fine St-Etienne side that Ipswich beat 7–2 – yes, 7–2 – on aggregate on their way to the final.

The game against Manchester City turned out to be his last game for Ipswich. After his glory days had ended he came to us at Colchester where his old centre-half from Portman Road, Allan Hunter, was then managing the side. I have a couple of abiding memories of him from that period.

The first came when we played at Watford in a friendly. Elton John had owned Watford for a few seasons and Graham Taylor was in the process of bringing them up from the Fourth Division into the old First Division. He was building the best team they ever had there with players such as John Barnes, Luther Blissett and Nigel Callaghan. They also had Ross Jenkins, a big centre-forward who played for them through all the divisions. He was 6ft 3in tall, which was remarkable at the time, and compared with the size of the defenders he played against he made Peter Crouch look like Wee Jimmie Krankie.

Even though it was only a pre-season match it was a big game for us. Watford played Graham Taylor's 'sophisticated' style of flowing football, their main tactic being to make sure the ball would 'flow' from the right- or left-back 40 or 50 yards on to Ross Jenkins's head. In the pre-match talk, our coach Cyril Lea was going through who was going to pick up who in open play and who would mark people at set plays. Obviously the question of who was going to mark Jenkins came up, but The Beat just said, 'Don't worry, leave him to me.'

When they stood side by side as the match started, you couldn't even see The Beat behind Jenkins – he was almost five inches shorter than him. But the first time the ball went up in the air for Jenkins to flick on, The Beat suddenly appeared above him as though he was bouncing on an invisible trampoline. The same thing happened on every occasion they tried to find Jenkins's head throughout the game. The Beat got there first and higher and did not lose a header in 90 minutes. It was all about his timing, his power, his athleticism. As a young player I just watched in awe: it was fantastic to see a player like that. He was thirty-whatever, with knees that were in big trouble and he was still jumping higher than any player I'd played with or against.

I was also thinking to myself, Cor, if we can keep him fit throughout the season, we've got half a chance. But the next pre-season game, at Leyton Orient, was in stark contrast. Everyone was getting ready to go out for a warm-up and a lot of players were going through the ritual of getting the match programme and going for a dump. It's either through nerves or because you think it makes you lighter for the game, and you'd always take the programme with you to read. The Beat disappeared into trap two and was in there for ten minutes. We were all ready to go out when he reappeared and called Cyril Lea over. 'Cige,' he said, 'you'd better write me off for this one.' Cyril asked what was wrong and Kevin replied, 'I'm injured.'

Cyril said, 'What do you mean, you're injured?'

The Beat, a legend in his own lifetime, replied, 'I was taking a dump and I strained too much and I've pulled a stomach muscle.'

We thought he was mucking about but he said, 'No, my stomach is killing me.'

He couldn't make it on to the pitch so someone had to take his place. Perhaps they should have given him Ex-Lax before the game. You could truly say that his Colchester career went down the pan.

Unfortunately, what happened after that wasn't so funny. Shortly afterwards, The Beat was to be seen signing autographs outside the DHSS in Ipswich – before going in to get his regular dole money. The building was so close to Portman Road he could see the new generation of players arriving at the ground in their flash motors.

The Beat has spoken about it publicly and also written his life story. He drank too much, was given the last rites in hospital once when his pancreas packed up and even contemplated suicide. He also became a carer for his seriously ill wife. Thankfully, he got his life back on the right track. I've met him since doing television work. He is a top man – not flash or bitter, but a man's man, no frills.

Quite a few of the players I discuss in this book can be glimpsed in action on the internet, including The Beat. But there is another place you can watch him in his prime if you go down to your local DVD rental store. Kevin was one of a clutch of English professionals who were used during the making of *Escape to Victory*, the film about how a group of Second World War prisoners planned to escape using a football match as their cover. It starred Michael Caine, Sylvester Stallone and, er, Pele. Bobby Moore and Osvaldo Ardiles were also in it, as were some Ipswich players. During one break in filming, muscle-bound 'Sly' Stallone challenged The Beat to an arm-wrestling bout. Stallone lost and didn't speak to Kevin for the rest of the shoot.

Unlike some of the footballers used, The Beat didn't have an acting role, but he was used in a lot of filming. If you think Michael Caine looks pretty useful in some of the movie's football action sequences, there's a pretty good reason for that. Kevin Beattie was his stand-in for those scenes. Not a lot of people know that.

CHAPTER 3

THIERRY HENRY

The first time I saw Thierry Henry was when he was playing for France in the 1998 World Cup. I thought he was crap.

France won the final, beating Brazil 3–0, but Henry didn't play for them in that game, even though he'd started or come on as substitute in most of their earlier games. True, he scored three goals to help get them there, but one was in a penalty shoot-out and the others were against South Africa and Saudi Arabia. He was playing up front and wide, and as far as I was concerned he looked out of his depth. He was ineffective, I thought his form was indifferent and he didn't have much to do with the outcome of the games at all.

He was only 20 at the time, mind, and the French did have a few guys in their side who could play a bit: Fabien Barthez in goal, Bixente Lizarazu, Laurent Blanc and

Marcel Desailly at the back, Didier Deschamps, Emmanuel Petit and Patrick Vieira in midfield, and they could always turn to a fella called Zinedine Zidane if the going got tough. Henry began the tournament in the starting line-up but ended it on the bench. It wasn't a bad bench to be sat on, though. At various times it had Patrick Vieira, Robert Pires, Frank Leboeuf and David Trezeguet on it. Nothing wrong with being a sub.

Obviously I didn't know anything about his track record. He was born in Paris in August 1977 and was given his debut for Monaco when he was just 17. The coach at the time there was a certain Arsene Wenger, who knows a thing or two about young players. Henry did well for Monaco, especially in the Champions League, and after that World Cup he went to Juventus in Italy. He didn't set the world on fire there, however, and only scored three goals in 16 appearances. Probably he hadn't matured as a player at that time. Wenger had wanted to bring him to Highbury all along; Henry was up for it too, so in August 1999 he arrived for around £10 million to replace Nicolas Anelka.

As a Gooner through and through, I couldn't help but think, What are we doing spending that amount of money on a Juventus reject who can't score goals? Obviously Arsene Wenger had a different point of view. 'Thierry Henry is a valuable addition to our squad,' he said. 'He is a young international striker who will be a great asset to Arsenal.'

Well, you don't need to be a genius to work out who was right and who was wrong there, do you? Move over, Arsene!

I wasn't the only one to have doubts, though. In Henry's first eight games he failed to find the mark and one newspaper labelled him 'The £10 million striker who couldn't hit a barn door'. Another said, 'He has blistering pace, great dribbling ability – but his shooting has been hopeless.' One tabloid journalist – I won't name him to save his blushes – assessed him like this: 'Manager Arsene Wenger bought him as Nicolas Anelka's replacement but he does not look to have the predatory instincts of a 20-goal-a-season man.' For accurate predicting, that must rate with Neville Chamberlain's 'Peace in our Time' statement a year before the Second World War began.

It wasn't until the third week of September that at last he started scoring. He came on as substitute for Kanu – it isn't just players like me who spent time on the bench – with 19 minutes left in a goalless game at Southampton. One wit said it was like bringing on Linford Christie to run the last 200 metres of someone else's marathon.

Henry could have walked off with a hat-trick. Southampton keeper Paul Jones made one great save from him and he missed with a simple header at the death, but with 12 minutes left he'd come up with a wonder goal. He had his back to goal when he received a pass from Tony Adams, then spun round in a split-second to bury a curling right-footed 22-yarder into the top corner. At the time I thought, Great goal – but was it a fluke? Eight years and 214 'flukes' for Arsenal later, I guess I'd got my answer.

To be fair, even Henry admitted after the Southampton game, 'I've played about eight games and I've missed about 14 chances. That goal was great for my confidence ... Before this, I played four years on the wing and then I'd maybe get only one goal in every four games. But now I have to work on my finishing. Goals for a striker are much more important in England.'

Arsene Wenger summed it up with a few prophetic words when he said, 'At the moment he is more comfortable on the wing, but I believe he can be more of a threat through the middle with his pace and power. He has the ability to play there – he's got all the natural qualities with his aerial power as well.'

You can say that again, although I'm not sure about the heading, Arsene.

Later in the week Arsenal had a Champions League tie at home – in fact, these games were played at Wembley – against the Swedish side AIK Solna. In front of almost 72,000 cold, wet spectators the score was 1–1 as the game entered injury time, a terrible state of affairs for Arsenal.

Henry had again come on as substitute – and managed to miss a sitter from eight yards – when he showed yet another glimpse of the talent the entire football world was to see in years to come. The fourth official had just indicated four minutes of added time when Arsenal launched what looked like a last, desperate attack. Nigel Winterburn's high ball forward was nudged on by Davor Suker to Kanu who, lying on the ground, dug the ball out and prodded it square for Henry. Lesser strikers would have trembled after that earlier sitter, but this time there was no reprieve. He slid home his shot in that soon-to-be-unmistakeable manner. To round off the night, he even laid on a third goal for Suker with virtually the last kick of the match.

'I did not panic when I missed,' he said afterwards. 'I looked up at the clock and saw there were 81 minutes gone and said to myself I had nine minutes to get the winner.' I think you call that True Grit.

'It was a relief when I scored. I have scored two very important goals for Arsenal, but I also remember I have missed a lot of goals against a lot of teams. If the coach asks me to be a central striker I will do it, but I will have to work even harder on the training ground to make sure I put away the chances I get. Don't forget I spent four years playing out wide. Maybe people think because I am quick I can get through the middle. There is more to it than that. I have to improve the timing of my runs from different angles.'

I know what you mean, Thierry.

I think I can say, without fear of contradiction, he did that all right. It was that move by Arsene Wenger from the wing into a central attacking role that was to change a very talented young player into one of the all-time greats.

Arsenal had a goal machine up front before Thierry Henry arrived in the shape of Ian Wright. Now I played with Wrighty and he was a terrific finisher, but he played very much down the middle. Most of Thierry Henry's best work was coming through the left-hand channel. It was Wenger's genius that saw the potential in that change of position for him, but being a manager isn't just about coaching, it's about making sure you have the right personnel available. Henry had the good fortune – make that the great fortune – to have Dennis Bergkamp up there with him when he started playing as a central striker. Wenger could see that they would be perfect for each other.

What a lot of people don't realise is that Henry was quite a physical player too. Not in the sense that, say, Ian Wright was – he wasn't the type to bundle through or just muscle defenders aside. But he's 6ft 2in and strongly built to go with his quickness. Looking at him you'd think his speed, which was frightening, was such he could have been an Olympic 100-metre runner, but he had the feet and the dexterity of another of my heroes, Tony Currie, and his movement meant he was a nightmare to face. When he was in full flow it was as though he was floating, but if you could get near him he had the strength to resist the challenge.

If you look at the number of goals he scored during his career, normally someone so prolific would be goal-sniffing chances in the six-yard box. But, out of the 200-plus goals that he got for Arsenal, I guarantee 140–150 of them would be great goals – running straight at people, chips, volleys, quality free-kicks.

Some of his free-kicks weren't just quality, they were inspired quick thinking too. Perhaps the best remembered is the one against Chelsea at Highbury in December 2004. It was a Sunday match and obviously it had massive implications for the title. It turned out to be one of those games that everyone describes as 'pulsating'.

It took Thierry Henry just 75 seconds to put Arsenal in front. A Jose Antonio Reyes header found him on the edge of the box and he controlled the ball with his right foot before lifting it into the corner of the net with his left. Chelsea equalised in the 17th minute when John Terry rose unmarked to head home Arjen Robben's corner, and the game carried on at that tempo with chances opening up at both ends. Then, in the 29th minute, came that controversial free-kick.

Chelsea, being the side they are, were still arguing about the free-kick being awarded (for a foul on Robert Pires just outside the box) as Henry stood over the ball. He had a quick word with referee Graham Poll and then Bob's your uncle – he calmly and fairly gently stroked the ball into the opposite side of the goal from their keeper Petr Cech, who was busy organising the wall. Talk about 'they don't like it up 'em'! The shit hit the fan there and then. The goal stood, though, no matter how much Chelsea protested and their manager Jose Mourinho moaned. Oh, the joy.

The game ended 2–2 but the main surprise was that Henry didn't manage to score a hat-trick. Even against a mean defence like Chelsea's – they only let in 15 goals in the league all season, which was the main reason they eventually won the title – he could have had a hatful.

Just to show that he was mortal – well, semi-mortal anyway – he managed to miss an open goal that even I would have put away. With a few minutes remaining, the goalkeeper had gone walkabout and, although there were couple of Chelsea defenders on the line, they were saying the last rites as the ball was gently and very invitingly rolled across the six-yard line by Robert Pires as Henry rushed in.

The fact that he somehow managed to put the ball high, wide and handsome with his left foot – easily done – made the miss almost as memorable as some of his goals.

The free-kick, however, was the talking point afterwards and, surprise, surprise, Jose Mourinho was none too pleased. 'I don't want to speak about it,' he said – and then went on to speak about it. 'If I do, maybe I have to go to the FA for a visit, maybe spend some time in the stands and spend some money that I'd rather spend on Christmas presents ... To say I'm unhappy would be a nice word. I can't say the word I hear in my head or feel in my heart, I just can't say it. I would like to say more because it was unbearable ... The result was fair and correct if you can forget about Arsenal's second goal. But for me it is difficult to forget about Arsenal's second goal, so I don't think the result is fair. There are the same rules all over the world – First Division, Second Division, China, Japan, Mexico, England – at every level of football of the game.'

Not surprisingly referee Graham Poll's verdict was somewhat different. 'The whistle doesn't need to be blown at a free-kick. I asked Henry whether he wanted a wall and he said, "Can I take it, please?" He was very polite. I deal with the laws and I deal with fact. I gave the signal for Henry to take it and that's what he did.' Read that bit again: 'Can I take it, *please*?' So Thierry Henry wasn't just a great player, he had impeccable manners too. What a gent.

It wasn't the first time he'd scored with a 'quickie' free-kick and his version of it all was dead simple. Poll had asked him if he wanted to take the kick quickly. 'The referee asked me if I wanted to wait for the whistle and ten yards. I said, "No," so he said, "You can have a go." I was just waiting for Eidur Gudjohnsen to get out of the way and the referee allowed me to do it.'

All sounds too easy to be true, doesn't it? I've no problems with goals from free-kicks taken quickly. If the players on the ball are thinking faster than the defending team, then good for them. Chelsea should have been more alive – it's as simple as that, especially as it was one of Thierry Henry's party pieces.

I wasn't too impressed, though, when Robert Pires once tried to roll a penalty to Henry against Manchester City. That was out of order, taking the piss, and it didn't help that they couldn't even do it properly and City managed to clear the ball. That was the pair of them trying to be a couple of Machiavellian 'French artists' but it just showed a lack of respect on their part.

Compared with some of the goals he scored while at Arsenal, that free-kick against Chelsea doesn't even get in Thierry Henry's top 50. I've mentioned that the vast majority of his goals were in the classic category as opposed to 'hit it and hope' or tap-ins. There would often be an air of inevitability about his intentions, especially when he was motoring in that left-hand channel.

I'm not going to run through all his great goals – that would need a book on its own – but there are a couple that I have to mention. No, I'm not talking about the trouncing of Charlton at Highbury that resulted in headlines praising 'Henry's Masterclass'. I know it was only Charlton's defence but, when Henry received the ball from Reyes with his back to goal, their big defender Jon Fortune was inches behind, not so much marking him as committing an indecent act in a public place. It didn't bother Henry – he just back-heeled the ball with as much power as some forwards get with a normal shot. As one critic said, 'It simply reeked of style, flair, imagination and sheer cheek.'

Nor am I going to go on about the volley and turn in between Denis Irwin and Gary Neville of Manchester United on the edge of their penalty area and the right-foot volley that flew high over Fabien Barthez's head before dipping under the bar.

But I am going to mention the third and final goal in the 3–1 FA Cup win over Liverpool at Anfield in January 2007. Henry, with possession in the centre of the field in his own half, passed the ball to the left wing – to himself. To be more accurate it was to a vast empty space down the left. He then set off after the ball giving ten yards' start to Jamie Carragher, an England defender (when he could be arsed). Henry gained on him with every stride as it looked like someone had tied Carragher's knees together, and when they both arrived at the ball at the same moment he forced Carragher off it and left him eating turf. That would have been enough for most men. You'd think he would have been happy to keep the ball on the left wing and wait for something to happen, but he had other things in mind. He roared on into the Liverpool area, turned a defender inside out and then hit his shot under their keeper Jerzy Dudek. Phenomenal.

It was almost as good as his solo effort in the 1–0 Champions League win over Real Madrid at the Bernabeu in 2006 – a wonder goal that made Arsenal the first English team to win there in any European competition. First Ronaldo and Mejia were shrugged aside, and Henry kept going even after Guti tried to assault him from behind. He finished his burst into the box by evading a despairing lunge from Sergio Ramos before unleashing his shot into the bottom corner. It was a goal that had to be seen to be believed.

'We did everything to try and stop Henry,' their centre-back Mejia said. 'We tried to push him, pull him and we tried to kick him but nothing worked. He was unstoppable. I've never seen anything like it. We tried to stop him by kicking him but he just came away still carrying the ball. The problem was Henry had already turned and he took us on one-by-one by running at pace. First, Ronaldo tried to get him but couldn't. That helped us to unbalance him. Then I tried to tackle him but he went over the top of me. Guti was next and he tried to take him down but Henry rode the challenge and kept his feet. He is so strong.'

I could go on and on describing Henry's fantastic goals, there are so many. But it is the quality that sticks in the memory. And note the names of the teams he scored against, Liverpool at Anfield, Real Madrid in Spain, Manchester United everywhere. He wasn't a playground bully – he delivered the goods against the very best time and time again. I rate him up there with the greatest because scoring goals is the hardest thing to do in football. It is a lot easier to destroy than create – that's why it's the goalscorers who fetch massive transfer fees and get the highest wages.

At the time that Arsenal let him go to Barcelona, a lot of people thought it was a mistake. But I think Arsene Wenger believed that his physicality had dropped and that, in a strange way, his heart wasn't there as it had been in earlier years. I thought he hadn't exerted the same influence as before in his last 12–18 months at the club, and he was now having a negative effect on the team. It was because he had become too big for the side – not on purpose, but because he had too great an influence on the young players all around him. Some of them were almost in awe of him, so once he went it allowed them to flourish.

Only two players, Alan Shearer and Andy Cole, have scored more goals in the Premiership. Only three players – Raul, Ruud van Nistelrooy and Andriy Shevchenko – have scored more goals in the Champions League. No one has scored more goals for France.

But great players aren't just statistics. They have a quality that you remember for years. The arrogant, 'look at me' gestures that Henry used to adopt after scoring yet another goal are as fresh now as the instant you saw him adopt them. I'm not criticising him for that, let me make that clear. All great players need that super-confidence in their abilities – it is an essential ingredient in their make-up. And if anyone was entitled to be proud of what he could do on a football pitch and the level of skill they could display it was undoubtedly Thierry Henry.

CHAPTER 4

TERRY HURLOCK

I'll never forget the first time I saw Terry Hurlock play. It was at Layer Road in Colchester, and when I saw him getting off the Brentford team bus before the game my instant reaction was that he looked like the Wild Man of Borneo.

He was wearing a massive loop earring, not something a lot of blokes did in those days, and he had this mass of hair you could get lost in for days. He always had the sort of hair that looked as though it had just had a bad perm, although Tel said it was natural and not down to a hairdresser. I for one wasn't going to argue. As I watched him lumber down the steps and off the coach, there was something about him that made you think of the real Guv'nor – Lenny McLean, the bare-knuckle fighter from London's East End.

I was a young apprentice at Colchester, and Brentford

were in a different division at the time, so it must have been a Cup competition that brought the sides together – I'm pretty sure it was the Milk Cup. Stan Bowles was in the same team as Tel, although Tel was just starting his career and Stan was finishing his after playing for bigger clubs such as Manchester City and Nottingham Forest. But it was his seven seasons at QPR that he'll always be remembered for, more so even than the five England caps he picked up along the way. Stan was recently voted the club's Player of the Century so you could see how much they adored him in that part of West London. He was also one of the first players ever to go public with his compulsion for gambling, something I've seen enough of in the game since then. He managed three years with Brentford before calling it a day in 1984.

He still looked pretty fit, mind you, and even though he was past his best the skill level he showed was awesome. He played to the crowd during the game and when a pass didn't find him would throw his arms up in the air as if to say, 'What am I doing here?' You couldn't blame him really.

Tel didn't have time for such showmanship. It wasn't his style anyway. He was born in Hackney in 1958 and started out as a schoolboy with West Ham, where he played with Alan Curbishley and Alvin Martin. He later said his problem as a teenager there was that he 'wanted to go out to pubs, clubs and dances'. That doesn't make him a bad person.

After a spell as an apprentice at the Hammers, he dropped into non-league football, playing for Leytonstone, Ilford and Enfield while he laboured on building sites, worked as a coalman and painted the white lines in the middle of roads. Not something today's Premiership players could even conceive of doing.

When he was 21, he signed for Brentford and he'd been there a couple of seasons when our paths crossed for the first time that day at Layer Road. I was just a kid and not in the first team yet, so I watched the game from the stands – thank God. It was obvious you didn't mess with him in midfield. He was so tough that years later I noticed that he looked hard in skin-tight leather strides – and that takes some doing. His reputation had come before him and it really was like having a bare-knuckle fighter against you in midfield. I was expecting him to behave like a Neanderthal man and he did bully the midfield, but I was surprised at just how well he could play. He had this presence about him: sure, he could handle himself but he couldn't half play too. I can't remember the result, but I remember thinking how good he was.

Tel never was what you'd call a publicity-seeking hard man like, say, Vinny Jones. I know Vinny and I'm not knocking him, but he built up this image of a hard man for himself. Good luck to him – it worked for him on the field and it worked out well when he finished playing too, but Terry was never into that. When Wimbledon played Millwall or Southampton and the two of them were on the field against each other, Vinny had more sense than to go near him. Some players go round saying, 'I'm going to break your leg,' but Tel didn't build himself up as an assassin – he just got on with it on the field where it counted.

Some players are famous for winning 50–50 balls: Tel would win 70–30 balls when he was the 30. He wouldn't start the trouble but if it happened he would be the one who finished it. When he went into a tackle it was like watching a wildebeest emerging from a cloud of dust after fighting with a rival.

After that day at Layer Road, we played in different divisions, so I didn't encounter him again for a few years. I'd been signed by Arsenal, while Tel had a brief spell at Reading before going to Millwall. But, by 1988/89, Millwall had somehow got into the old First Division for the first time in their 103-year history. I say 'somehow' but they actually had a good side, one of the best in their history. Up front they had a very young Teddy Sheringham and their main goalscorer was Tony Cascarino, who was Ireland's centre-forward for years. They were even near the top of the table chasing Liverpool and Arsenal when they came to Highbury at the start of March – they eventually finished a very respectable tenth.

They brought a massive load of fans with them – the docks must have been shut for the day – and they hammered us. They played us off the park, yet the result was 0–0. The pitch that day was in a terrible state with more sand on it than in a circus ring. They had Les Briley in midfield alongside Tel. Les was running round topping everyone and Tel was running round smashing everyone. I was on the pitch from start to finish for once and normally if things were going quiet I'd start looking for the ball, wandering inside. But with Terry in the middle I thought discretion was the better part of valour and stayed out wide.

Les Briley then scored a perfectly good goal but for some reason the linesman had his flag up. No one knew why it was disallowed. I'm not sure even the ref did, but his linesman had flagged – I think because their winger Kevin O'Callaghan was standing alongside him – and that was that. No goal. But no way was he interfering with play. Their manager John Docherty said afterwards he had no idea who was offside, but whoever it was must have been on the pitch – at White Hart Lane.

The decision didn't just cost Millwall maximum points: in a way it enabled Arsenal to win the league championship. It was nearing the end of the season and there wouldn't have been too much time left for us to make up any ground we lost. We ended up winning the title at Anfield on the final day of the season on goals scored with virtually the same team who played against Millwall that day. So Briley's disallowed goal would have made all the difference as we would have had one less point at the end of the season.

Early in his career Tel earned himself the nicknames of 'Gypo' – because of that earring – and 'Animal' – after the crazed drummer in *The Muppet Show* – because of the barnet. The Millwall fans decided to call him Terry Warlock and someone even wrote a poem about him. I won't repeat it all, but the opening lines go:

'They called him Gypo, I preferred *God*
Built like a labourer carrying a hod
But when he played, he gave it all
That's Terry Hurlock, of Millwall.'

Yep, I know whoever wrote it won't get the Poet Laureate job when it comes around again, but it just shows how much they loved him down at the old Den. He's listed in their Hall of Fame on the official club website.

There's even some footage of David Beckham playing against Terry when, as a youngster, Becks was loaned by Manchester United to Preston North End for a month to toughen him up. This is how he remembers it: 'It was a month I look back on with good memories. I once scored from a corner and played against Terry Hurlock, which was quite interesting. I stayed away from him as much as possible.' No fool Beckham, then.

In August 1990, at the age of 31, Terry went to Rangers for £300,000, joining the big English contingent that manager Graeme Souness had assembled there – Chris Woods, Terry Butcher, Gary Stevens, Trevor Steven, Mark Hateley, Nigel Spackman and Mark Walters. Tel was only in Scotland for about a year, but they loved him up there – he was their type of player. He was one of three Englishmen – Mark Hateley and Mark Walters were the others – who were sent off in one game against Celtic.

When we later ended up playing at Southampton together, Tel told me a story about his days up in Scotland. Although he was now playing on the south coast of England, he still had a home in Scotland – for the simple reason he couldn't find anyone to buy it. 'Bloodnut,' he said – that was his name for me because of my red hair – 'the estate agent has done me up like a French rat.'

It seems the house he and his wife Kath had been shown

was lovely: four bedrooms, lots of space, fitted kitchen and bathrooms. In those days it would be like Beckingham Palace is now. They said yes on the spot, without looking in the garden. It was only after they moved in that they noticed a noise coming from there. When they looked out, all they could see was a big, fuck-off-sized electricity pylon going 'zizz, zizz, zizz'.

'No wonder the agent never opened the back door when he showed us around,' Tel said.

When he invited people round he was worried that they might get some form of radiation sickness! He ended up selling it for about £30,000 less than he'd paid for it. He's no Robbie Fowler, who ended up owning an entire street of houses.

It was during his three seasons at Southampton that I got to know Tel well.

Southampton people don't like outsiders, especially London people. Even some of the local players were insular. That meant that me and Tel, both having London connections, sort of got together – that and the fact we both liked a sherbet.

The conversation would go something like: 'Fancy a light ale, Bloodnut?' and I would always answer, 'Why not, big fella?'

We ended up living near each other in Chandler's Ford, near Southampton. I spent most of my time at the club trying to recover from a bad injury and for a period he was injured too. At least that meant that we were free to get on with the drinking.

We'd meet up for a drink about 12.30pm at a pub in

Chandler's Ford and we'd tell our wives we'd be back a little later for some lunch. Later on we'd call to say we'd be back for tea and it usually ended around 9.15pm, having fish and chips back at his place. He'd say, 'Do you fancy a bit of Elve?' and start playing his Elvis Presley collection. That was all right by me – I'm an Elvis fan too.

During his time at Millwall, Terry had played three times for England B, against Switzerland, Iceland and Norway. He'd even got a goal in one of them. It might not be the greatest international career ever, but don't say that to Tel. He is as proud as punch over those appearances.

When you play for England, you get a tracksuit and all the gear, and he would wear that tracksuit for training at Southampton. Now with some players you might think they were being flash bastards, but not Tel. He was just so proud of that tracksuit and what it represented. 'Three lions, Bloodnut,' he would say to me and point to them on his chest, 'three lions.' He really was proud to be English. He respected people like the Chelsea Pensioners, the old guys who'd fought for their country, and he admired passing-out parades. A lot of people sneer at events like that, but not Tel.

Most people who remember him think of him as a really large guy. But he is only 5ft 9in, average height really. It's just that he was built like an outhouse door and, with his hair and the way he played, he somehow gave the impression he was a giant.

Tel is, in fact, a gentleman. He really is. He's got this gypsy/Romany image but it was only when someone took what he would call 'a diabolical liberty' that he would act on it. Once you got to know him you couldn't help but like him – he is very down to earth and one of the funniest men I've ever met. But it's a mistake to get on the wrong side of him.

We used to go to a pub called the Captain's Table for a drink. We were in there on a Tuesday when a big local hard man came in with his mates. He came up to Tel and said, 'You're Terry Hurlock, aren't you?'

Terry said, 'Yeah, chief, that's me.' I think Terry thought he just wanted a chat or something.

Then the guy said, 'I hear you're a bit of a nonce in the showers with the young boys.'

I just thought, Oh fuck, here we go. In Tel's book that was the worst insult you could get. To be called a nonce, a man who's got a thing about young boys, was as bad as it gets.

Tel just said, 'What did you say?'

The guy repeated it, and Terry went to grab hold of him but somehow the landlord managed to split them up. Half of me was glad that he did, because who needs trouble when you're having a drink? I'm a lover not a fighter. But the other half of me reckoned that the guy really needed teaching a lesson. Tel just turned to me and said, 'Bloodnut, things like that I don't let go.'

Now it so happened that we were playing my old club Arsenal at home that Saturday. I'd broken my toe and wasn't fully recovered, so I was sub (there's a shock). That meant I was heavily involved in sorting out the other players' tickets for their guests, and Tel had about 20 he wanted handing out. That was a lot but, when I asked him why he needed so many, he just said, 'I've got a bit of an entourage coming down.'

Stupid me – I thought that, as they were all Londoners, they probably wanted to watch the Arsenal.

Southampton managed to beat the Gunners 2–0 – thanks in part to the information I gave them about my old club's tactics.

Paul Merson was playing and he had permission to stay down rather than go back with the team to London. That meant we'd be having a few sherbets after the game. 'Where shall we go?' I asked Tel.

'I fancy a light ale in the Captain's Table,' he said. 'A few of my mates are coming down.'

I should have suspected something there and then. By the time I got down to the pub there were a group of heavies in the corner. Half of them looked as though they'd done time and the other half looked as though they were on their way to doing some. Tel introduced me to them all and I said it was nice to meet them and so on.

Merse then came in but soon left with a bird from the office, so he was out of the way – and then two Southampton hard men came in, including the one who'd been out of order earlier in the week. Tel did say to me, 'If you want to make yourself scarce…' but I said, 'No, in for a penny in for a pound.'

You could say there was a bit of an atmosphere – and then two more Southampton so-called tough guys turned up. The bolts went on the doors and within no time there were bodies everywhere. It was like a scene out of a Western. As a famous Norwegian commentator might have put it, 'Southampton, England, your boys took one hell of a beating.' Pretty soon there were sirens going as the police arrived, and a couple of Tel's mates grabbed us and ushered us out and away from the police. Later on I met up with Merse in a nightclub called New York's.

The next day there was a massive story in the papers about 'Top England stars caught in bar-room brawl' all over the front page. It named me and Tel, Merse and Nigel Winterburn. Well, two of us were there but Merse had left by the time the trouble started. And, as for Nigel Winterburn, he'd got straight on the team coach after the match and headed straight back to London, so he had a perfect alibi. It seems that one of Tel's 17-stone mates had needed some hospital treatment and been asked his name. He just said, 'Nigel Winterburn,' and that's how it got out.

Merse got it in the neck from George Graham but as always he got one more last chance. It was more of the 'You and Perry Groves, when you two get together ...' But Merse and Nigel had the last laugh, as the paper had to pay damages to the pair of them, as they hadn't been involved in a brawl at all. I guess it all went to show that it didn't play to mess around with Terry Hurlock, the hardest man I ever met on the pitch – and pretty tasty off it too when pushed.

Tel had three seasons at Southampton before going to Fulham. During his time at Craven Cottage, Tel – who was continually booked and sent off seven times during his career – managed to amass a club record 62 disciplinary points in one season, so the flame still burned bright. But he broke a leg badly in a pre-season friendly against Brentford of all teams, and after that bad injury he decided to call it a day. 'I'll be 36 next year so I think it's time to knock it on the head,' he said. 'The injury is taking a long time to mend. My contract runs out at the end of the season and I don't think I'll be staying in football, although I may play a few amateur games just to keep fit.'

The Times newspaper once published a list of the hardest men in football and Terry came in number 23. All I can say is, I'm glad I didn't have to play against any of the other 22.

CHAPTER 5

JOHAN CRUYFF

It was the evening of 19 June 1974 and Jan Olsson was about to enter football history; 53,700 fans were packed into the football stadium in Dortmund to watch 32 year-old Olsson and his Swedish countrymen take part in a World Cup finals first-round match. He'd already played in the 1970 finals in Mexico, so by the time the German tournament came around four years later he was an experienced international defender.

In case you're wondering why Jan's name isn't ringing any bells, don't worry. I had to look it up too. Although Olsson's moment of fame is constantly seen on television and the internet, he wasn't the star of the show. In fact, he was the fall guy, the stooge, the patsy. It was Olsson's bad luck to be in the wrong place at the wrong time. Sweden were playing Holland, the Total Football team of the tournament. They had a stunning squad including Johnny

Rep, Rene and Willy van de Kerkhof, Arie Haan, Ruud Krol and Johan Neeskens, and many say they deserve the title Best Team Never to Win the World Cup.

And best of them all was the man who humiliated poor old Olsson – who played for humble Atvidabergs FF in the Swedish league – that night, Hendrik Johannes Cruijff. You probably know him as Johan Cruyff – it's spelled differently outside Holland – the man who was to be voted European Player of the Century two decades later and who had so much natural talent it just wasn't fair on the rest of us.

Olsson, no mug as the Swedes had a good team, moved to tackle Cruyff just outside the left side of the penalty box. Just to make sure the Dutchman wasn't going anywhere he gave him a little tug on his shirt. Cruyff, who had his back to goal, didn't seem to have the ball totally under control as he looked up and made as if to pass it into the area with his right foot. Instead he wrapped his instep around the ball, slid it behind his standing leg and accelerated away, having completed a 180-degree turn. It all happened in the blink of an eye. Football folklore had a new chapter – the Cruyff turn.

Olsson must have wished he'd stayed behind to enjoy the Swedish lakes and pine forests instead of becoming Cruyff's plaything. The poor guy helped complete the memorable image by looking for a moment at where Cruyff and the ball should have been, staggering like he'd been on too much vodka before finally – when he half-realised what had happened – turning to give chase. By this time he was so off balance the best he could manage was a stumble like an OAP on roller skates.

If you ask anyone to name a football move by one player, some fans would mention Cristiano Ronaldo's step-overs. Some might go for Colombian goalkeeper Rene Higuita's scorpion-kick, and others might choose Maradona and his keepie-uppies. But the clear winner would be the Cruyff turn. I don't know if he ever trademarked it, but he should have.

And it wasn't a fluke, as he went on to do it again. This time it was the Brazilians who suffered. Talk about the biter bit. That was later in the tournament in a game that was to decide who would go through to the final, so it wasn't just a case of showing off against lesser opposition. It was just part of the Cruyff repertoire.

One critic called him 'Pythagoras in boots', adding, 'Few have been able to exact, both physically and mentally, such mesmeric control on a match from one penalty area to another.' Took the words right out of my mouth.

That World Cup was my first real glimpse of Cruyff, but the guys he was playing against shouldn't have been too surprised. It wasn't as though he was a new kid on the block – he was playing for Barcelona by that time and had previously been a star with Ajax.

Cruyff was a greengrocer's son who was born in Amsterdam in 1947 close to the Ajax ground where his mother was a cleaner. She often washed the players' shirts and persuaded the coaches to admit her son to their youth development system at the age of 12. An English coach, Vic Buckingham, recommended that the club sign him on a contract and he made his first-team debut at the age of 17. Naturally he scored.

He became a teenage sensation and two years later he was playing for Holland, scoring a late equaliser in a 2–2 draw with Hungary. At this time – the middle and late 1960s – Dutch football was largely amateur but change was coming and Cruyff was to be a key figure in the transition.

If he was the figurehead on the field, the Dutch had a brilliant coach off it – a man called Rinus Michels, who became manager of Ajax in 1964. Within a few years his side was to become the best in the world. Throughout their glory years, Ajax relied heavily on home-grown talent. Many of them, like Cruyff, weren't just Dutch but also had grown up near the ground, and all had been nurtured by a remarkable youth scheme.

One of the first to receive a taste of what lay ahead was Bill Shankly's mighty Liverpool, who were thrashed 5–1 in a 1967 European Cup match. By 1968, Ajax had won a hat-trick of Dutch championships and the following year they reached the final of the European Cup, only to lose to AC Milan. To complete the transformation, Ajax – an amateur club just a decade earlier – won three European Cups on the trot. Panathinaikos, Inter and Juventus were beaten finalists in 1971, 1972 and 1973 and the long-striding Cruyff, his arms out for perfect balance, was the star in every game.

He didn't score in the first victory against Panathinaikos but he ran the show, and he got both goals against Inter in the second win. The only surprise about the third victory was that it was by such a narrow score – trust the Italians to hang on in there. But there were periods when Ajax tore them apart in front of a crowd of

93,000 in Belgrade and one football encyclopaedia said later, 'He inspired one of the greatest 20-minute spells of football ever seen as Ajax overcame Juventus 1–0.'

In that 1971/72 season, Cruyff was voted European Footballer of the Year. He had been the top scorer in the European Cup with five goals, as well as being the leading marksman in Holland with 25 league goals. In September 1972, Ajax, with Johan Neeskens and Rudi Krol added to their galaxy of talent, also won the World Clubs Cup, beating the South American champions Independiente 4–1 on aggregate, and the first European Super Cup with a 6–3 aggregate victory over Rangers.

Even as a young player with Ajax, Cruyff was outspoken about money. In the late 1960s, it was very rare for a Dutch player to move around Europe, let alone cross the Atlantic. Yet when it was suggested that he might be bought by a South American club he said in one interview, 'Of course I want to go. This is not to say I want to leave Ajax, or Holland. But I must think ahead to a time when I can no longer play football. I must prepare now for myself and my family. I'm very happy, but I want to go for the money. Nothing else. [Never heard that admitted by a player before or since.]

'I pay SEVENTY per cent of my earnings in tax. This is ridiculous! In South America I would pay only a very small percentage of that. If I am seriously injured playing for my country, there is no insurance money for my wife. And if I miss a club match because of illness or injury my wages drop to a very low level. Every time I asked about this, I am told, "Ah, Cruyff is shouting again. He is getting too big." Then they tell me the public don't want me to leave. I say all the fans can give me one guilder each – that's about two shillings and sixpence [twelve and a half pence for you youngsters!] – and I'll stay. I want a better contract so that I can put money away for the future. But, if the club refuse to release me, I'll stay and do my best for them.'

He was also outspoken about the way the game should be played – with some views you wouldn't expect from a Dutchman in the 1970s. 'In these four years as a professional I have seen and learned four types of football. The English play fast and high; the Dutch are skilful but too soft; and the South Europeans – the Spanish and the Italians – build up slowly with assured moves. To me, the English way is best. People say they are dirty. They are not – just hard. Certainly, they have one or two dirty players, but so have we and we know who they are. But we in Holland must develop a hard approach to the game.' He even liked the English!

Cruyff was voted European Footballer of the Year for the second time in 1973. At the end of that season he left Ajax to join Rinus Michels, who was by then in charge at Barcelona. Cruyff cost a world record £922,300 and would be followed by Neeskens, who signed for Barça during the 1974 World Cup finals.

The Spanish season had already started by the time Cruyff arrived and the Catalans were struggling down the table. He soon changed all that. First of all he said he would never dream of playing for Real Madrid because of their links with the dictator General Franco. That made him an instant hit with the Catalans who support Barcelona. On the pitch they rocketed up the table and won the championship, including handing out a 5–0 thrashing to Real in Madrid.

That 'hard approach' Cruyff that had called for helped Holland beat their rivals Belgium to qualify for the World Cup group stages in 1974. It also meant some hard negotiations over pay, as the national team reckoned they weren't getting enough money. Another example of Cruyff's appreciation of what his name was worth came when he took the third black stripe off his Adidas-sponsored Holland football shirt. He was sponsored by Puma, so he didn't want to promote a rival firm. Brand Beckham had nothing on our Johan.

But I didn't care about any of that as a nine-year-old watching the Dutch strut their stuff in Germany. I was mesmerised, like kids all over the world, watching football as I'd never seen it played before.

Holland's first opponents were Uruguay, who tried to boot them, especially Cruyff, off the park. They failed, and Holland won 2–0. Despite Jan Olsson being turned into a human corkscrew, the Swedes came out of their group game with a valuable point after a goalless draw, but then Holland thrashed Bulgaria 4–1.

If Holland – coached by Michels – had been superb in the first round, they were brilliant in the second. In those days the two finalists were the teams who finished top of the second-stage mini-leagues, and the Dutch were in a tough group with Brazil, Argentina and East Germany.

As always, the Argies had a decent side, but, even with

the South American Player of the Year Ruben Ayala, the British-born Rene Houseman and a very young Mario Kempes, they were humiliated by the Dutch. Cruyff put the Dutch ahead when he pulled down a shoulder-high ball, skipped round the keeper and slid the ball home from an acute angle with his left foot. Despite playing the match in a downpour, Krol, Rep and Cruyff added further goals to make it 4–0 in a complete attacking display.

The East Germans were then beaten 2–0 and that meant the winner of the Brazil–Holland game would go through to the final, making it effectively a World Cup semi-final.

One observer at that game wrote, 'The Brazilian defence kicked, chopped and hacked from the first; and it must be said that the Dutch, thus provoked, returned the treatment with interest ... In the first half, Neeskens was knocked cold by Mario Marinho. In the second, he was scythed down by Luis Pereira.' But it didn't make any difference to the Dutch – they were out of this world. Cruyff made one goal for Neeskens in the second half and then volleyed home a second soon after. In between he showed us the Cruyff turn again. And why not?

Everyone, apart from those wearing lederhosen and with names like Wolfgang or Fritz, wanted the Dutch to beat the Germans in the final. The Dutch stroked the ball around for well over a minute at the start of the game and then won a penalty when Cruyff was fouled as he raced into the box. The Germans hadn't even touched the ball yet as the English referee, Jack Taylor, a butcher from Wolverhampton, awarded a penalty. The Germans got level with a penalty of their own and Gerd Muller scored the winner. Cruyff even managed to get himself booked at half-time by choosing to have a go at Jack Taylor. Well, he never was backward in coming forward.

Cruyff might not have got himself a winner's medal, but he was voted the player of the tournament (he also won his third European Player of the Year award). It was the last time he appeared in a World Cup final, however, as he retired from international football before the 1978 tournament in Argentina. Some people said he didn't go because he didn't approve of the Argentinean military junta of the time, but Cruyff himself said he did not want to be separated from his family for such a long period again. Years later he said they had been targeted by a gang of kidnappers and he was concerned for their safety.

In 48 games for Holland he scored 33 goals, a remarkable ratio for a man who was not an out and out striker. In fact, he was as far away from a traditional centre-forward as you could get. For a start, he always wore the number 14, as he'd worn it early in his career when he was returning from injury as a squad player and felt it brought him luck. He'd often come deep or go wide on the wings – the reality was that he played wherever he felt like it.

This was his verdict on the Total Football he played: 'Sure, we never won the World Cup but everybody keeps asking, "Did you try to be too entertaining?" How can you ever be too entertaining? In my view, if you are being entertaining, you are simply playing well and if you are playing well you will score a lot more goals than you are letting in. Sure, by playing this way there will be bad games, and sometimes you might doubt the way you play. But you must stick with it.

'While I think too much is made about formations and not enough in the drop in technique throughout football, I have always been a 4-3-3 man. I have never played 4-5-1 and never would. Why? Simply because, with 4-3-3, it's easier to make combinations going forward. With only one up front, who is he feeding off, passing to? Football is about having the best offensive play possible and 4-3-3 does not have to leave you exposed.'

However, the great German defender Franz Beckenbauer had a different take on Total Football. 'It owed more to the element of surprise than to any magic formula. I think the Dutch got away with it for so long because the opposition could not work out what tactics they were facing. It never dawned on them, certainly not until it was too late, that there were no tactics at all, just brilliant players with a ball.' So perceptive, Franz.

Soon after that 1978 World Cup, Cruyff went to America and played for Los Angeles Aztecs and Washington Diplomats, followed by a brief spell at Levante in Spain. Eventually, the prodigal son returned to Ajax, by then a shadow of the great team they had been only a few years before. With Cruyff back in their colours, Ajax won the Dutch championship twice in two years. During this spell, he famously scored by rolling a penalty to team-mate Jesper Olsen, who pushed it back to him, leaving the goalkeeper stranded. Cruyff then tapped it in the net. As I've mentioned, Robert Pires and Thierry

Henry famously tried to do this in a league match for Arsenal against Manchester City and ballsed it up. Cruyff, who would have been nearly 60 then, could have done a better job.

But this Indian summer at Ajax wasn't to last. His original deal was reportedly linked to the gates he attracted but after two years he couldn't agree contract terms with them: he wanted his salary to reflect the increase in the gate money. The result was that the unthinkable happened: in 1983 he signed for bitter rivals Feyenoord of Rotterdam, where he could get the slice of the gate that he wanted. He knew that the extra people in the crowd had come to see him play. I've no problem with any of that. That's him knowing his worth and he was one of the first footballers to realise his commercial value. 'It was as if the Pope had become a Jehovah's Witness,' said one observer, but even the Pope's got a price.

Cruyff's brilliance continued and Feyenoord won the league for the first time in ten years, completing a league and cup double in the process. And to think he did all this while smoking at least 20 cigarettes a day throughout his career! It wasn't until the 1990s that he saw the error of his ways, and that was after a double heart-bypass operation. I can excuse most vices, but smoking – I hate it.

In 1986, Cruyff returned to Ajax as manager and in his second season they won the European Cup Winners' Cup. After that he moved on to Barcelona, where he became the longest-serving and most successful manager in their history with 11 trophies, including their first European Cup. Once that was theirs, Cruyff was the King of

Catalonia. By 1994, Barcelona had won four successive Spanish championships but the next couple of years were trophy-less and in 1996 he was sacked in favour of former England manager Bobby Robson.

Cruyff remains one of the few great players in football to become successful in management. At Barcelona, a lot of training sessions consisted of playing two-touch football, six against four, in an area half the size of the penalty area. 'In a small area,' Cruyff said, 'the movement is necessarily fast and the passes must be pinpoint. Two of the six play wide and change team whenever the other four gain possession. It is always six with the ball against four trying to retrieve it. This possession principle should operate in any area of the normal field of play, so our training is intense and is the basis of our game. You can close down space more effectively by accurate passing when you have the ball, forcing opponents into certain positions, than you can by man-marking without the ball.'

Cruyff had been a great passer of the ball so now he was trying to instil the same quality in his side so that the man receiving the ball can escape his marker.

'This ability is controlled not by the receiver but by the passer. The passer can see the field in a way the receiver cannot. If the receiver has his back to goal, the passer should send the ball to the foot on the side where the receiver should turn, reducing the arc through which he must control the ball to move.' Simple.

And he showed that he had lost none of his powers of observation when he pointed out to one interviewer: 'The great strength of the English game, which worries all foreigners, is its pace, the quick movement of the ball forward. But midfield carries the balance of every match. Control the midfield and you control the game. So long as English teams allow themselves to be outnumbered in midfield they will not exploit their advantages.

'The main problem in Britain is that there are too many competitions and too many games. There is no time to prepare properly for Europe or to introduce new ideas because there is far too much emphasis on domestic football.'

The key stage of any footballer's career, Cruyff maintains, is when they are aged about 12. 'At that age, you know whether or not a boy is going to be a player. There are fundamental skills, which you have or don't have, which cannot be taught after that age.'

He obviously made sure his son Jordi was brought up the right way as he ended up playing for Barcelona and Manchester United. He didn't have 'Cruyff' on his shirt, though, just 'Jordi'. It must be a right bastard having a father as famous as that if you're a footballer. It doesn't matter what you do, people will always say, 'He's not as good as his father.' Still, it must have been great to be taught the Cruyff turn by the man himself.

CHAPTER 6

ANDERS LIMPAR

The 1989/90 season was probably the best of my career. Although Arsenal finished fourth in Division One after winning it a year earlier, I thought I'd played well, either up front or out wide on the left. At the age of 24, I reckoned I was playing the best football of my life and I was hoping to establish myself in the team. Then Anders Limpar came along and put the mockers on everything.

That title of ours 12 months earlier – won at Liverpool on the last day of the season – was picked up by a virtually all-English side and that certainly isn't going to happen again in a hurry. Nowadays, foreigners are joining English clubs practically every hour. The signings are never secret, most of the negotiations seem to be conducted on the sports pages and the arrival of a new player from overseas is announced a long time in advance. But it was different then, very different.

Anders appeared practically out of the blue as far as I was concerned. Our manager George Graham realised he had to bring in new players, so he made three £1 million signings in the summer of 1990: David Seaman from QPR, central defender Andy Linighan from Norwich – neither of whom was going to keep me out of the side – and Anders.

He started his career in Sweden but moved to Switzerland with the Young Boys Club of Bern and then on to Cremonese in Italy, so I didn't know much about him, even though he'd been in the excellent Swedish squad for the 1990 World Cup finals in Italy. He joined us on pre-season tour, coincidentally in Sweden. There was a great team spirit at the club and we were a fairly young squad, so of course we welcomed them on board. 'Where do you play?' I asked Anders, and he said, 'Left side…' Please let him say left full-back, I thought to myself, but he paused for a second and then said, 'How do you say in English?' The agony continued until he eventually finished the sentence by saying '…left wing.'

Bollocks! I thought. The gaffer's not bought him to play in the reserves, has he? Still, you have to get on with it, so I gave him a forced smile, a bit like Tony Blair meeting someone he can't stand the sight of but pretends he wants to be their bestest friend. 'Great,' I said, shaking his hand. 'Hope it all works out for you. See ya.' Then I walked away and said to myself, 'Better get my cushion out again and put it on the bench…'

I then started to think what every player thinks when someone comes in who plays in their position: All right –

how good are you then? I want to see what you can do. Let's see if you really are better than me... Then I saw him in training and my heart sank. Fuck me, I thought, he *is* good. I'm going to have a year being his stuntman. As always, that was very perceptive of me because that's exactly what happened. If he was away on international duty I'd get a game in the Rumbelows Cup or something like that but he was definitely above me in the pecking order.

But it was an inspired signing, because he transformed Arsenal from being a very good side into a great one and, despite my fears, I still took part in 32 of the 38 league games we played on the way to winning the title – 13 from the start and 19 coming on as sub. Much as it sticks in my throat to say it, I've got to admit that it was a good move on George's part. Nevertheless, with my starts and sub appearances, I still got a decent look in that year.

As he was a foreigner, albeit one who spoke the language really well, we needed to introduce him to a few old English customs. When he arrived at Arsenal, Anders was virtually teetotal, so of course one of the first things we did was take him out for a drink. The Tuesday Club was the name we gave our weekly drinking club – assuming we didn't have a midweek match – and we would go to a variety of places for the day and night, as long as they sold alcohol. To introduce Anders to one of our haunts, we went to AJ's in Mill Hill in North London, not far from our training ground. It was where we had taken Jimmy Carter when he was signed from Liverpool and he managed to piss down my and Paul Merson's trousers.

Well, there might be a few piss artists in Sweden who could have given us a run for our money, but Anders definitely wasn't one of them. After four bottles of Heineken he started talking Swahili and then it was 'Good night and God bless'. He would always say to us, 'Imagine how fit you'd be if you didn't drink,' and I suppose he had a point. But it's not as though we were at a disadvantage: every club had a drinking culture so why should we be an exception? Anyway, we had better players, which is why we won things.

That first season Anders was at Highbury we won the championship and he was fantastic. We were so good as a team in that 1990/91 season that we won the title seven points ahead of runners-up Liverpool. That was despite having two points deducted because of a brawl in our match with Manchester United and having our captain Tony Adams jailed for a drink-driving offence halfway through the season. We only lost once in the league – away at Chelsea – all season.

Anders may only have had little trotters for feet and very little back-lift before letting go, but he had real power in his shooting. You'd watch him in training and you'd think, Fuck me, he's good. Left foot, right foot, it didn't matter. But then you think, OK, this is happening in training, but what's it going to be like in proper games? It didn't take long to find out when he scored his first goal for the club.

Arsenal were in a four-team pre-season tournament at Wembley involving Aston Villa, Real Sociedad and Sampdoria. Our first game was against Villa, and I was watching it, from the bench of course. With just over half an hour gone, Anders went down the left wing, checked and cut inside. He was still only six or seven yards from the touchline but suddenly he bent the ball with the outside of his left foot and just smashed a shot past the goalkeeper's left hand and into the far corner.

All right, I thought. It was a great goal, but it was only pre-season. It's not big boys' football, after all! But he turned it on everywhere that season. Grounds don't come much bigger than Old Trafford and he scored a great goal there in October 1990. We had a corner on our right just before half-time and the ball was tapped to Anders. He was practically on the by-line and with his back to goal, but he half-turned to face the goal and in that instant saw United's goalkeeper Les Sealey was at his far post.

Anders didn't hesitate: he just bent his shot low and hard towards the near post with his left foot from the most acute of angles. Sealey scrambled across and flicked it out, but it had gone over the line. A few of their players went through the motions and protested it hadn't – well, they would, wouldn't they? – but the referee Keith Hackett was in a perfect position and didn't bottle it. It was a great goal and the kind of thing that elevated Anders to a higher level: he had the vision to score a goal like that but also the confidence to try to score from that position at a place like Old Trafford.

The game will best be remembered, though, for the brawl that broke out in the second half. Anders – who'd been embarrassing them by nutmegging their players – and our full-back Nigel Winterburn were in at the start of it, while Brian McClair, who tried to kick lumps out of Nigel's back while he was on the ground, and Denis Irwin were there for United. A four-man brawl is pretty good, but that was just the start.

Pretty soon 21 players were involved – David Seaman decided he couldn't be bothered – and both sets of benches went on the pitch too. As a sub, I couldn't stop laughing at it all. Anders ended up being shoved into the hoardings at the side of the pitch by a United player, which was the nearest they came to tackling him all game. Both clubs and loads of players on either side were later fined, and George Graham came up with the clever idea of getting Arsenal to fine him as well – it sent out the right message about Arsenal and the behaviour expected of everyone at the club.

It was great stuff, though, and you can relive it on YouTube any time you like. It might have happened years ago, but that punch-up is always high up whenever a list of best ever football brawls is drawn up. Strange to think that Anders, who's only a little chap, and those nutmegs of his were the catalyst not just for that brawl but also for the element of needle that exists between the two sides to this day.

As for nutmegging opponents, some people think it's taking the piss, but I don't. I think it's brilliant if you're good enough to do it. On the occasions that I used to do it, I'd shout, 'Whey!' as I went past the defender, just to rub it in. If you're a spectator paying £50 or £60 to go and watch a game, I think that's what you want to see. You've paid a lot of money and you want to see something that ordinary players just can't do. It's not showing disrespect, it's showing skill. I suppose your feelings about it are governed by who's doing it. If it's a player on your team it's wonderful; if it's an opponent then it's an absolute liberty.

Anders made 39 appearances in all competitions that season, plus a couple as sub, and got 13 goals in total. He wasn't our leading scorer, but he would find the net against the best. You could never call him someone who just turned it on against the lesser teams, either. He was that good they were all the same to him. He's not like, say, Ronaldo at Manchester United who can tear mediocre sides apart and show all the tricks in the book and then some, but struggles against the top sides.

That goal by Anders at Old Trafford shows what I mean, and the next season he scored an even more memorable goal when we hammered Liverpool 4–0 at Highbury. He gathered the ball in his own half, moved quickly into theirs, shuffled a bit, gave a little shimmy, moved the ball on to his right foot just past the centre circle and noticed the keeper was off his line. The next thing anyone knew he'd lobbed their goalie from 40 yards and it was in the net.

It's not just me who rates him either. George Graham didn't see eye-to-eye with him towards the end of his time at Arsenal, but he has said of Anders that when he came to the club, 'He was probably the most exciting player in the English league. He had flair, he was quick over five yards, so quick, two good feet and a magnificent shot.'

Ian Wright, one of the best goalscorers in Arsenal's history, went so far as to say that in his early days at the club 95 per cent of his goals were created by Anders.

The funny thing is that, if you asked an Arsenal fan today to draw up a list of club legends, Anders probably wouldn't be anywhere near the top. The reason for that is simply that, despite that fantastic first season, he wasn't at the club long enough to have as much impact as his quality deserved.

In his second season Anders struggled, because we struggled as a team. He was not a grafter, and in one sense he was a luxury player. He could be out of this world for 20 minutes and then that was that. It was fine when the team were on fire as we were in the championship year, but not when things weren't going as well.

George Graham said at the time of Anders's subsequent move to Everton, 'Anders needs a new challenge. He is coming to the end of his contract and he deserves the chance of regular first-team football. He is one of the most talented players I have coached but he has not been able to transfer that ability on to the pitch on a regular basis. He has been a very popular player with the fans and I wish him all the best.'

I have my own take on that. I'd moved on to Southampton by then and perhaps having the safety net of his stuntman removed meant that he went down a gear. Well, it's a theory, isn't it?

Our paths crossed while I was at Southampton and he was still at the Gunners. They came down to play us and I was the spy in the camp. I knew all the Arsenal moves and strategies: what they planned at corners and free-kicks, their strengths and weaknesses. I practically did the team talk for our manager Ian Branfoot: how they would take people away at near-post corners, how one man would peel away to the far post and one to the near post, how at free-kicks they would put three men on the end of the opposition wall, how defenders and midfield might show you inside...

I ran through all the technical stuff but, when it got to Anders and the best way to nullify him, I just said, 'Boot him.' I said our defenders should larrup him in the first few minutes just to let him know they were there. It's not that he couldn't take that sort of stuff, it's just that no one likes it, so it would put him off his game a bit.

I'd been out with a broken toe so I was sub for the match, but I came on for the last 25 minutes or so and got a really good reception from visiting Arsenal fans, which was quite touching really. I was playing wide on the right and Anders was playing on the left so we were opposite each other as soon as I came on to the pitch. We'd got on very well at Highbury and as I ran on the pitch he shook my hand.

A little later we had a goal kick, so Anders dropped back to cover the midfield near me and I heard him saying urgently, 'Perry! Perry!'

What did he want? 'All right, Anders?' I said.

Then he said, 'After the game, we swap shirts?'

I was about to say it was fine with me when the ball flew over our heads and on to Iain Dowie, who was busy knocking it down so someone, namely me, could run on to it. Instead of being there to support him, I was talking about shirts with Anders!

He was such a top player that I was thrilled that he wanted to change shirts with me but in those days it wasn't the done thing unless it was a Cup Final or European match. If you swapped your shirt at the end of a game, the kit man would kill you!

Anders was at Highbury when Arsenal beat Sheffield Wednesday twice to win the FA Cup and League Cup in 1993. He didn't figure in all those Wembley games, but his time with the club was drawing to a close. In March 1994, he was transferred to Everton for £1.6 million, after turning down the chance of going to Manchester City. Even though it was late in the season, he'd only figured in a dozen Arsenal games so it was the right move for him at the age of 28. He was promised first-team football at Goodison, which he wasn't getting at Highbury by that stage. Arsenal were inconsistent and so was Anders. When a team are struggling, you need more grafters and Anders wasn't that type of player. The flair players there had become a liability.

Everton had a great team in the middle and late 1980s, but they'd gone off the boil by the time Anders joined them – they were getting old. Only Arsenal had been in the top division longer than Everton, but that year they had to wait until the last game of the season before they avoided the drop. Anders almost dropped them in it when he gave away a penalty, when, for no reason other than he felt like it, he decided to clear a Wimbledon corner with his hand. 'I had a brainstorm,' he said. 'I couldn't reach the ball with my head and instinctively I stuck up my hand. I felt gutted for the fans and when we went two down I couldn't see a way out of it for us.'

Despite being 2–0 down, Everton managed to win 3–2 and avoid the drop. The following year he was outstanding when he helped Everton win the FA Cup by beating the favourites Manchester United 1–0. Anders was also part of the Swedish squad who finished third in the World Cup in America in 1994.

But it wasn't long before he was on the move again. He'd been unsettled for some time at Everton when in January 1997 Trevor Francis, the Birmingham City manager, signed him until the end of the season for £100,000. That too ended in tears after four games when he was fined for failing to turn up for a reserve match and his contract was annulled.

'There was an element of risk when we took Limpar from Everton,' Francis said. 'His ability and technique were never in question but he has had one or two problems with other managers concerning commitment. I felt he may have provided us with that extra bit of quality we needed. Rather than let him hang around until the end of the season, I decided it was better if he was released from his contract now.'

After that Anders went back to Sweden to play for AIK in Stockholm for two years before heading for Colorado Rapids in America's Major League Soccer. He spent a couple of years there before returning to Europe and signing for another Stockholm club, Djurgarden. You'd hardly think that would set anyone's pulse racing, but by then Anders was running a bar in the city called The Limp Bar – another original name – and the AIK fans didn't like him signing for their local rivals. They spat at poor old Anders, called him a 'traitor' and smashed up the bar. He finally called it a day in 2002, saying his body couldn't take it any more. I know the feeling.

I've mentioned other people in the game, such as George Graham and Ian Wright, who also rated Anders highly. But there was also one little kid who idolised him during his time at Everton. This lad would imagine he was Anders as he kicked a ball around with his mates near his little home in Croxteth in Liverpool, often reliving that 1–0 Cup Final victory over Manchester United. The boy's name? Wayne Rooney.

CHAPTER 7

TEOFILO CUBILLAS

The summer of 1978 was one of those World Cups where you had to watch Scotland as England had ballsed it up again and not got to the finals for the second time on the trot. Poland had knocked us out in 1974 and this time we'd failed to get there as Italy had a better goal difference in their qualifying group.

English people can watch Scotland and not give a shit whether they win or lose because we know we're better than the Jocks. But when the Scots or Irish or Welsh watch England play they are desperate for England to lose. They hate us. It's not like that with the English. We support other British nations when they are playing. If they win it's 'fine'; if they lose it's 'so what?' It's a bit like watching the tennis player Andy Murray; if he wins he's British, if he loses he's Scottish.

That meant that in 1978 in Argentina we were

'supporting' Scotland and Ally's Tartan Army. The 'army' was named after their manager Ally MacLeod. When he'd taken over the side he'd told all the players, 'I'm a winner,' and he stated before setting off for the finals in Argentina that his side would come back 'with at least a medal'. Asked what he would do after the World Cup, he replied, 'Retain it.' Oh dear.

So optimistic was the feeling among all those lovely Scots lads that they even released a song called 'Ally's Army' which included the words, 'We'll really shake them up, when we win the World Cup, because Scotland is the greatest football team.' It got to number six in the charts. The Scots even had an open-top bus tour *before* the tournament and 25,000 turned up at Hampden Park to watch as the players were driven around the stadium waving to the crowd. Prestwick Airport was besieged by fans eager to see them depart, and Scots from all over the world headed to New York and turned left to watch their side in Argentina. One critic said the nation was 'gripped by collective madness'.

Nothing wrong with a bit of optimism, and in spite of all the bollocks they did have some quality players in Kenny Dalglish, Graeme Souness (both of whom had just won the European Cup with Liverpool), Martin Buchan, Joe Jordan, John Robertson and Archie Gemmill. So they were no mugs, but they seemed to ignore the fact that Brazil, Holland, West Germany and Argentina, to name but a few, were pretty useful too. So was Teofilo Juan Cubillas Arizaga of Peru.

The Scots were hot favourites to win their first match

when they took on Peru but history has shown Scotland
– who've never got past the first round of a World Cup
final – are inevitably the team who get home before their
postcards. Cubillas was the man who would hammer the
first nails in their coffin.

I hadn't heard of him before the game but Cubillas was
already an established star in South America. He was
born on 8 March 1949 near Puente Piedra, and is held in
the same regard in Peru as Pele is in Brazil, Maradona in
Argentina and Zidane in France. Known in Peru as 'Nene'
(or baby, for his baby-faced appearance), he started his
career at Alianza Lima at the age of 16, making his debut
in 1966.

During his first stint at Alianza, he scored 116 goals in
175 games, was the Peruvian league's top scorer in 1966
and 1970, Libertadores' top scorer, and South American
Footballer of the Year in 1972. All that is pretty
impressive, especially as he was a midfielder, but it was to
be a World Cup that made him a star, because in those
days it was practically the only global platform they could
perform on as very few South Americans came to Europe
to make their name.

That 1970 World Cup tournament in Mexico is thought
by many to be the best ever – if you leave out England's
1966 win, that is. England were still strong, perhaps even
better than the side of four years earlier. Germany under
Beckenbauer were a force to be reckoned with, Italy had a
host of stars and of course there was Brazil.

It was in this company that Cubillas made a name for
himself while still a youngster. He scored four goals in the

first round – one against Bulgaria, two against Morocco and one against West Germany – and helped Peru into the quarter-finals. There they had the misfortune to meet Pele and his pals in all their pomp. Brazil won 4–2 but Cubillas scored again and returned home a hero, complete with the tournament's Young Player Bronze Boot. As the two young players ahead of him were Brazil's Jairzinho and West Germany's Gerd Muller, he'd certainly made his mark. He was even included in the All Star side.

In 1973, he moved to Europe, but not to one of the glamour Spanish or Italian sides – he went to Basel in Switzerland. Although he scored seven goals in 14 games, he'd never lived abroad before and found it difficult to settle. So he moved to Porto in Portugal where the climate and the culture were a bit more like home and where he scored 65 goals in 108 games. He also starred in the Peru side that won the inaugural Copa America trophy for Central and South American sides for the only time in their history. In 1977, he returned to Peru for a second stint with Alianza Lima and scored 42 goals in 56 appearances. Remember when you look at this goal tally that he was a midfield player, not a striker.

And so to 1978. Nowadays you get all the European and South American football on the box here, so you get to know the star players. Back in those days the South Americans were unknown to us apart from their appearances in the World Cup, so unless your name was Pele, Maradona or Jairzinho you were a complete unknown. Perhaps Scotland hadn't done their homework all that well on the 29-year-old before the kick-off on a lovely evening in Cordoba on 3 June 1978.

I was so excited. There were very few live games on back in the 1970s. You'd have the Cup Final, the Home Internationals, perhaps a very few England internationals and that was it. This was a bonus. It was summer, there was no other football on, and here was the World Cup beamed live into my living room. To watch a live game from the other side of the world was unbelievable. What 13-year-old football-mad kid wouldn't want to watch it? The time difference meant it was a really late kick-off by UK time but my dad had told me I could stay up and watch it.

I still wanted Scotland to win rather than Peru. I knew who the players were – they were British after all – and I had a passing interest in seeing how well they would do in the tournament. Peru? They were just one of the minnows of South American football and the country was only known for llamas, Incas and Paddington Bear (who was from 'deepest, darkest Peru', remember?).

I sat down to watch it and expected Scotland to give them a hammering, to win by three or four goals. Sure enough, after 14 minutes, Joe Jordan gave them the lead. But this was Scotland. It was bound to end in tears, as it always does. The Peruvians looked really comfortable on the ball and none more so than Cubillas. He wore the number ten shirt – which meant he must be their best player – and he even looked like Pele. A lot of people referred to him as 'the poor man's Pele'. You can take that one of two ways, I guess. Me, I consider it a compliment.

I've mentioned some of the players in that Scottish squad, but one I haven't got round to was their curly-haired goalkeeper Alan 'Home Perm' Rough. In fact, a more accurate comparison would be with Deirdre of *Coronation Street*, as they both had the sort of twisted, corkscrew barnet that lives terrifyingly on in the memory.

Rough played for Partick Thistle and was the latest in the line of, shall we say, memorable Scottish goalkeepers. Anyway, the Scots had got off to a great start when Joe Jordan gave them that lead. But as all those Jocks in the 38,000 crowd started singing and dancing they might not have noticed that the Peruvians were stroking the ball around like a team who really knew what they were doing. Every time they ran at the Scots' defence they looked like causing problems.

David Coleman, who was commentating on the match for the BBC, said ominously, 'Peru have got real ability in attack,' and alongside him Bobby Charlton added, 'They have been threatening to score every time they come near the box.'

Sure enough, Cubillas flicked a lovely little pass in the penalty area to Cueto who equalised just before half-time.

It wouldn't be Scotland without a hard-luck story, would it? Although Peru were playing them off the park by this time, the Jocks could have gone ahead in the second half but Don Masson had his penalty saved by the Peru goalkeeper.

Then Cubillas really strode on to centre stage. In the 72nd minute, the Scots allowed him too much space just outside the area and he pulled back that right foot of his

Bobby Moore and Pele, 1970. Perhaps Pele was telling him: 'I don't want to see my shirt on eBay.'

'1966 and all that – Mooreo's finest hour.'

Terry Hurlock. No opponent in sight – shock!'

Above: Ronaldo: 'I want my mummy.'

Below: Eric Cantona: 'Have you got these boots in another size?'

Above: Thierry Henry: 'Je suis magnifique.'

Below: Alan Shearer: 'Putting his foot through it, as he did 260 times in the Premiership.'

Above: Ronaldinho: 'A great player – and that's the tooth.'

Below: Peter Shilton to one of his defenders: 'Oi, you! It was your fault.'

The name's Beckenbauer, Franz Beckenbauer.' *Der Kaiser* dressed to thrill.

Johan Cruyff thinking: 'I can feel a funny turn coming on.'

and the next thing poor old 'Deirdre' knew was that he was picking the ball out of the net. That was pretty sensational, but there was even better to come – from a Peruvian point of view, that is.

The South Americans were given a free-kick on the edge of the penalty area just to the left of the box. 'The Peruvians are pretty useful from these dead-ball positions,' dear old David Coleman told us. Visionary, Dave.

The Scots got their wall of blue shirts all lined up nicely as Cubillas ran up to the ball virtually dead straight, not at an angle. Then he bent his shot with the outside of his right foot and it went into the net high to the right of the goalkeeper. It wasn't actually Rough's fault – he even got his fingertips to it. It was a great goal and not one of the famous Scottish goalkeeper howlers. I guess Rough didn't come up against shooting like that very often against teams like Hamilton Academicals and St Johnstone. In fairness to him, it would have beaten a keeper from any club in the world. He must have thought, That's not allowed – I set my wall up for someone bending it with the instep, not the outside of their foot.

I had never seen anyone take a free-kick with the outside of their foot before. The next day I was out in the back garden in my Gola Nova trainers with an orange stripe, an orange Wembley Trophy ball – I was quite ginga-biased – and our springer spaniel Duke in goal. Duke was as alert as 'Deirdre' and had a better barnet as well – all his curls were natural. I didn't actually break my toes, but I smashed them a few times trying to kick a dead ball like Cubillas had.

Given that this was my first glimpse of Cubillas, why do I choose him as one of my all-time favourites? The answer is that my judgement is based on the impact that players have on you. It seemed so exotic to watch a game from the other side of the world and settle down to watch Dalglish, Gemmill and Masson – and then someone you've never heard of emerges who does something completely different.

Cubillas wasn't just a dead-ball player. His all-round game was superb, his passing and reading of the game was faultless and he was very graceful on the ball. I've always maintained that the number ten seem to be the best player in the team and he was another example of that.

The Scotland captain that day, Bruce Rioch, still remembers him, as well he might. 'Your man Cubillas hit that wonderful free-kick,' he said in one interview. 'It was a devastating result and we all felt it. I still get a wee shiver when I hear Cubillas's name. He was a fantastic player and he was the man who put us to the sword that day.'

'Deirdre' remembers it even better! 'Ultimately, Argentina 78 was only billed as a disaster because we had done so well in the qualifying process and had a team full of really top-drawer stars,' he said on one anniversary of the match. 'But right from the start we suffered a major blow, when Gordon McQueen, who was our key central defender, was injured and failed to make it. Then, of course, we met a Peru side that no one had heard of in our first group match and, well, they blew us away.

'With guys like Teofilo Cubillas, and his ability to bend free-kicks with the outside of his boot, they had players who had skills we just didn't have in Britain. In fact, 30 years down the line, that free-kick he put past me is still giving me nightmares!'

Things went from bad to worse for the poor old Jocks. First their winger Willie Johnston failed the after-match drugs test. Medication for hay fever was the cause, the Scots said, but he was still sent home in disgrace never to play for his country again. Then came a truly terrible result. In their next game the Scots could only draw 1–1 with Iran. That meant they had to beat Holland by a hatful to qualify for the next stage. They managed to win 3–2 and Gemmill scored a memorable goal, but it was too little too late, so off they went for their customary early trip home. I shed no tears for them. Surely it was obvious they weren't going to win the World Cup, especially as they'd been beaten by the fifth-best team in South America?

Peru actually topped their group – Cubillas scoring a hat-trick in their victory over Iran – but lost all three games in the next group. Their final game is one of the most controversial in World Cup history. Under the tournament structure Argentina needed to beat Peru by a large margin to have a better goal difference than Brazil and make it into the final. Surprise, surprise, that's exactly what they did, putting six of the best past Peru's Argentina-born goalkeeper. There were also murmurings of visits to Peru's dressing room by Argentinean government officials.

Peru made it to the 1982 World Cup finals in Spain but, although Cubillas played in all their three games, he was past his best by then. He retired from international football soon after and ended his career playing in the States – as everyone seemed to in the 1970s and 1980s – but his total of ten goals in the World Cup final stages still puts him seventh in the tournament's all-time scorers.

And it isn't just me who rates him, by the way. In 2004, Cubillas made it into the FIFA List of 100 Greatest Players of All Time. The man who compiled the list? A certain former footballer by the name of Pele.

CHAPTER 8

PETER SHILTON

I first became aware of Peter Shilton when he kept goal for England against Poland at Wembley on 17 October 1973. It was, as it always seems to be, a 'must-win' game for England if they wanted to qualify for the World Cup finals in Germany the following year and Sir Alf Ramsey's side were expected to be too good for the Poles. I was eight years old and watched the match at home with my dad, praying that England would do the business.

Shilts wasn't having much to do that night while at the other end Jan Tomaszewski – famously called a 'clown' by Brian Clough before the match – had been performing miracles for the visitors. Remember, these were the days before we all had Polish plumbers. As far as we were concerned, they spoke a funny language, came from the back of some East European beyond and were there purely so we could give them a football lesson.

England were all over Poland and with all that pressure it seemed inevitable that a goal would come, so there wasn't much to worry about as Grzegorz Lato broke down the left in the 57th minute. Norman Hunter went across to close him down near the halfway line and in the normal course of events 'Bite Yer Legs' would probably have sent him back behind the Iron Curtain in several bloodstained pieces. Unfortunately, the Leeds United defender must have left his killer instincts back at Elland Road as he decided to gently usher the ball out of play like a ballet dancer doing warm-up exercises. He missed the ball and Lato too, and off went the bald little bastard at high speed.

Even when he passed to Jan Domarski there wasn't much danger. He got his low shot in before Emlyn Hughes could tackle him, but it was pretty close to Shilton and wasn't exactly travelling at the speed of sound. Most goalkeepers would have been happy to just block the shot or push it away. But Shilton wasn't an ordinary goalkeeper – it wasn't in his nature. As he himself said years later, he decided to 'make the perfect save'. All well and good apart from one fact – he missed the ball. Instead of simply getting in the way of the shot, he tried to grab the ball in those big arms of his, only for it to go under his body. Not quite what I would call 'perfect'. Cue Polish delight and English misery. England managed to equalise from the penalty spot – about the only way they were going to score that night – but the draw meant it was an England exit from the World Cup. Exit Alf Ramsey soon afterwards too.

Even Hunter had to confess, 'Peter Shilton should have thrown his cap on it. The shot wasn't brilliant but it went under him. He should have really saved it, but it was my fault. I've never played in a more one-sided game and lost.'

They weren't the only ones gutted. Imagine how I felt as a young kid having to pretend to support Scotland at the finals in Germany the next year. So you'd think I might have a little bit of bad feeling towards Shilton, but how could I? He really was one of the greats.

Whenever anyone starts discussing who was the best goalkeeper ever to play for England it always boils down to a 'Shilton vs Banks' argument. There's no one else apart from Shilton up there alongside Banksie, and the way things are going with the shortage of quality English keepers, it's going to be a while before someone comes along to make the argument a bit more interesting.

Banks and Shilton – the names seem to go together. It's not surprising really. Shilton – who narrowly gets my vote – had been Banks's protégé and followed him into the Leicester and then England goal, earning the great man's seal of approval. He even followed him at Stoke City. I know a guy who went to the same Leicester youth club as Shilton when they were both aged about 11. My pal wanted to be a goalkeeper but was told, 'We've already got one of those.' Then Shilts appeared. He looked years older than he was and dwarfed all the kids around him. It wasn't long before he was training with Leicester's youth team and by his mid-teens he'd filled out to become a six-footer, and was already turning into 14-stone-plus of muscle. Now for a boy to take on youngsters five years older than him like Shilton did is remarkable, it really is, even if the guy is a goalie.

Shilton was such a prodigy that he made his debut in goal for Leicester at the age of just 16 in May 1966 – before England's World Cup win that summer when Banks was one of its stars – and he kept a clean sheet against Everton. After that he had a career that most footballers can only dream of.

It lasted 30 years, during which he won a record 125 caps – including 66 clean sheets – but it could, and should, have been a lot more. For a long time his main rival for the job was Ray Clemence and at one stage they even alternated games under some barmy take-it-in-turns rota system. Now Clemence was a good keeper too, but not in Shilton's league if you ask me, so if you take into account the 61 caps he won, not to mention the nine that Manchester City's Joe Corrigan picked up on the way, and give them to Shilts – well, you do the maths.

Shilton didn't make his first appearance in the World Cup finals until 1982 – as England had failed to qualify for two tournaments running – but he more than made up for his late start. He then played in 17 games in the finals, more than any other Englishman, and kept a clean sheet in ten of them.

Shilts also notched up over 1,000 league games and is the only man to have made more than 100 league appearances for five clubs (Leicester, Nottingham Forest, Stoke, Southampton and Derby). He was first-choice keeper at Leicester from the age of 17 and he was so good they decided to let Gordon Banks move on to make way for him. Later, he too moved to Stoke City for a world record fee for a goalkeeper of, wait for it, £300,000 – it was a lot of money back in those days, honest – before Brian Clough took him to Nottingham Forest. Old Big 'Ead might have got it wrong about that Polish goalkeeper but he got it spot on with Shilton. With him in goal Forest won the league and then the European Cup two years running. Cloughie said Shilton was worth 10 to 15 points a season to Forest, and he was right.

Shilton was the first goalie that I was really aware of. Until then the goalie was just the fat kid you put in goal because he wasn't much good in any other position. It didn't matter too much, because if your side was good enough then the opposition wouldn't get as far as your goalkeeper anyway! Well, I did say I was only eight.

I remember watching Shilton for Forest on *Match of the Day* and he would make a run-of-the-mill save look as though it was something out of Barnum and Bailey Circus. He'd tip the ball over the bar and the way he landed was fantastic: he'd bounce on one foot, bounce on the other and then flip himself back. It was almost as if he was diving twice – once to make the save and the second dive to regain his balance and position and make it look difficult.

Shilton took goalkeeping to another level. In the 1960s, 1970s and 1980s, there were no specialised goalkeeping coaches. Of course, being in goal was different from playing outfield but it was Shilton who led the way in its becoming a specialist position with its own training routine and work. Before he came along goalkeepers would train by simply taking crosses, stopping shots and booting the ball upfield. Even then you'd still see keepers kick a ball straight out of play. I mean, how can you kick a ball out of your hands towards a pitch 120 yards long by 75 yards wide and still manage not to keep it on the park? Well, they did a lot of that. Shilton moved it all on to another plane. He brought a stringent regime to his training and worked on every aspect of his game.

He was so good he even had a clone – John 'Budgie' Burridge. If it's true all goalkeepers are mad, then Budgie was probably the craziest of the lot. He used to go to bed at night wearing goalkeeping gloves and take a ball with him, just so he could feel it. When England played at home he'd go along with his boots and gloves in a kit-bag, just in case all the selected goalies got injured or were taken ill. He obviously believed in the 'Is there a doctor in the house?' theory and that, at the last minute, he'd be asked to go in goal to help England in a crisis.

Like Shilton, he played professional football for almost 30 years and, also like him, he worked out and was a training fanatic. Come to think of it, he even looked a bit like him. He wasn't as good as Shilts, though. I'm not doing him down by saying that, because you don't earn a living playing football for that length of time unless you're pretty good at what you're doing, but he didn't have Shilton's class. He did have a career to match Shilton's in other ways, mind. He played for a record 15 clubs in the English league, and he's still the oldest man to play in the Premiership after he turned out for Manchester City at the grand old age of 43.

Given that Budgie was around so long, it's not surprising that our paths crossed. Arsenal were playing Southampton and he was in goal for the Saints. My job was to stand in front of the keeper at free-kicks or corners and just try to get in his way or deflect the ball – anything to annoy him. Nowadays the keepers put their arms up and draw attention to the fact they are being blocked but Budgie had a different technique. He just stamped on me with his massive boot and broke my toe. The pain! I turned round to square up to him and he immediately yelled, 'Ref! Ref!' so it looked as though I was the one who'd started the trouble. The instant that he did it, I thought – You fucking twat, but I must admit afterwards I thought – That was smart of him. Now that's the sort of thing you can't coach youngsters, is it?

But I digress. Peter Shilton's England career ended after the World Cup in Italy in 1990. He then became a goalkeeping coach for England for a while. That didn't last too long, but he did coach David Seaman when he was starting out with the England set-up. Dave ended up with 75 caps – second only to Shilton – but he didn't think too much of Shilts's training methods. He'd come back to Arsenal from a session with the England squad and say 'fucking works too hard'.

What he was saying was that Shilton's methods might have been all right for Shilton as a player, but they didn't necessarily work for everyone. Perhaps that's why it didn't quite work out for Shilts when he went into management: he wanted everyone to be in his own mirror image and it doesn't always work out like that. It's also difficult for a goalkeeper to become a good manager. I can think of Dino Zoff who was a great Italian keeper for years and a decent manager, but no one else springs to mind. It's simply that they spend their careers in their specialised position so it's very hard for them to understand the problems of other positions.

There were a number of areas of the goalkeeping art that Shilton brought to a higher level than they'd been before.

To begin with there was agility. Of course there had been mobile keepers before, but no one like Shilton. Remember he was a big guy and you don't automatically associate big men with agility. That went out of the window with Shilts. There's a famous photograph of him making a save for England against Scotland at Wembley. How he got near Kenny Dalglish's shot high to his left through a packed penalty area was a miracle in itself, but in mid-air he realised he wouldn't be able to reach the ball with his left hand. That would have been that for most goalkeepers, but Shilts twisted his body and somehow reached the ball with his right – his 'wrong' hand – and had enough strength in it to push it clear. It was over in the blink of an eye – it actually takes longer to describe than it took in real time.

He was also a master of narrowing angles and making it difficult for the forward to decide where to shoot. That meant any hesitation by the guy trying to score would be fatal – at the level he played at, either Shilton would get him or a defender would.

He also was one of the first goalkeepers to 'make himself big' in a one-on-one situation with an attacker. Probably the most famous exponent of this intimidating art in the modern game was Peter Schmeichel of Manchester United. He was even bigger than Shilts and he'd thunder out of his goal like some bozo blond Viking, putting the fear of God into the poor sod he was heading for. Well, Shilton was doing that 25 years earlier; he practically invented it. He reversed the traditional role of a centre-forward accelerating towards a terrified goalkeeper. The way Shilts perfected it, the goalkeeper practically became the attacker and the man with the ball at his feet was on the defensive. You didn't want 14 stone of prime Leicestershire beef clattering into you if you could help it.

Shilton was also a forerunner in dominating the penalty area. You read a lot about it nowadays, but if ever they show any old footage of him on the box or you see clips of him on the internet you'll see what I mean. The box was his domain: anyone else seemed to be an intruder. That went for defenders as well as the opposition. You just got out of the way if you had any sense when he decided to come for the ball. There was one exception, but I'll get to that later.

But his greatest gift to the goalkeeping repertoire, his legacy to all those who followed in his footsteps and those still waiting to put on a pair of gigantic padded gloves, would place him in my Hall of Fame on its own. Simply put, it is this: always blame your defence for the goals you let in.

When a goal was conceded BS (Before Shilton), the keeper would simply turn around and pick it out of the net. Perhaps, just perhaps, he might give a sad shake of the head and his shoulders might sag a little, but that was it. If the goalkeeper was to blame? There was a hand immediately held up in the air to acknowledge the mistake, and perhaps even a 'sorry' to his team-mates. Shilts changed all that.

No matter how a goal has been conceded – whether the ball has been smashed into the top corner with unstoppable power or it has trickled pathetically through the keeper's legs – the reaction now is universal. Goalkeepers the world over immediately pick themselves up off the floor, select the nearest defender, take a step or two towards him and point a finger vigorously at him. This is always accompanied by a mouthful of abuse aimed at the man he's selected. The keeper makes sure that the crowd inside the stadium and whoever is watching on TV get the point: he wasn't to blame – it was the other guy, he was the one who was crap.

Oh yeah, and don't forget the final, very important gesture. The defender might have a go back at the keeper and blame him, but, as the entire defence walks away getting ready to start the game again, the keeper must turn and face the net – and the spectators behind it – shake his head and hold his arms out with his palms upwards. His whole body then sends out the message: what kind of twats am I dealing with here?

If Shilts didn't invent this manoeuvre, he certainly turned it into a fine art. He was the Godfather of 'Weren't My Fault'. He was a legend for most of his long career, so, if he made it clear someone else was to blame, who would question him?

I remember him playing for Derby against the Gunners at Highbury. Someone crossed from the right and he misjudged it, got too far underneath it and the ball ended up in the far corner of the net. There was no wind in Highbury that day, not even the slightest breeze. If Dawn French's knickers had been hanging on the line they wouldn't even have twitched, but that didn't stop Shilts.

For the next five minutes he was at the edge of his area bending down to pick up blades of grass. Then he'd gently throw them in the air above his head, like a golfer before a key shot or a rugby player judging the strength of the wind as he's about to attempt a conversion. He'd make a half-moon shape with his hand as if to show how strong the wind was and how it was carrying the grass away. All this was with just one thing in mind: that the uninitiated would think it must have been the wind that caught the ball and took it over his head. Me and Steve Bould saw what he was doing, but the other 39,998 must have thought, Poor old Shilts – he didn't have a chance once the wind caught the ball. What a pro!

He wasn't quite as professional in one aspect of his private life, though. I was in my mid-teens when I picked up the newspapers one day and found out that Shilts – a married 'Mr Clean' – had been discovered in his car one night with a bird who wasn't his wife. Shilts had met her in a nightclub and gone for a curry with her, and in the small hours of the next morning the two of them were found in his car by the bird's husband. Shilton drove off in his Daimler, only to hit into a lamp-post which promptly fell on top of his car. When the police arrived he was cut to the face and, more to the point, almost two times above the legal limit for drink-driving. The result? A 15-month driving ban and a £350 fine.

It just so happened that his first game after all this became public was at Highbury against Arsenal. Just to make him feel at home the crowd sang, to the tune of 'Bread of Heaven', 'Peter Shilton, Peter Shilton, Does your missus know you're here? Does your missus know you're here?' And, to round off a perfect week for him, Arsenal won 1–0 and pictures later showed that the ball hadn't crossed the line. Shilts had, of course, protested, but when your luck's out...

Even at my early age, I made a few 'notes to self' from the events of that week. First of all, if you are going to be alongside another man's wife in a motor, try not to park under a bright streetlight where he can spot you when he goes for a drive to find out why she ain't home yet. Second, if your car is involved in an accident, then report it stolen – but make sure you say it was nicked about three hours earlier. Third, and most importantly, if you do get caught, make sure she's an absolute darling – it's not worth it otherwise.

It also emerged later that Shilts, like a lot of players I know, liked a flutter. The trouble was that most of the horses he backed are probably still running. He spoke about it publicly, though, and admitted he had a problem – the main one being he was a crap punter – so he faced up to it in the end.

But time catches up with us all. When Shilts played for England in those 1990 World Cup finals, he was the oldest man in the competition at 40 and I think it showed in the end. In the semi-final against West Germany, the one where Gazza cried – for himself – the Germans scored a goal that I'm sure a younger Shilton would have stopped. Andreas Brehme's free-kick took a terrible deflection off Paul Parker's arse, the ball ballooned up into the air and seemed to be there a long time before it looped over Shilts and into the net. It looked as though he was wearing lead diving boots compared with the Peter Shilton of five or so years earlier, who'd have done a Wayne Sleep pirouette and tipped it over the bar.

I'm not slagging off one of my all-time heroes, but you don't want him to be remembered for something like that. Perhaps it's like being a professional boxer; you're always the one who is last to know that it's time to call it a day.

But let's remember the facts: in between that Polish goal at Wembley in 1973 and the semi final against the Germans, this man played at the very highest level for 27 years. It is astonishing, a tribute to all the hard work he put in to top up his natural ability. But he knows better than anyone that keepers are best remembered for their mistakes, not all the saves they made. Perhaps only Gordon Banks with THAT save from Pele's header is the exception to the rule.

The final irony for Shilton, though, is that the incident for which he will be most remembered is another goal that went past him. It's the one image captured on camera that has been looked at more than any other in his career. True to form, he immediately protested it wasn't his fault – and this time he was right.

The game in question was the quarter-final of the World Cup in 1986 in Mexico between England and Argentina. There was no score six minutes into the second half when that horrible little Argie Diego Maradona began running at the England defence. His pass was off-target but Steve Hodge, who had intercepted it, sliced the ball up in the air. Maradona's run had taken him past Hodge into the penalty area – and into the path of the ball. Shilts came out ready to punch it clear but then Maradona, all 5ft 5in of him, got there first and flicked it into the net. It wasn't via his head, though – as we all know, it was his left hand that got there first.

Shilts and the rest of the England guys immediately appealed for handball, but the Tunisian referee, Ali Bin Nasser, apparently didn't see a thing and one of the most famous quotes in sport was made by Maradona after his country's 2–1 victory. He was asked how the goal was scored and he said, 'A little with the head of Maradona and a little with the hand of God.'

Shilts at least managed to put it in plain English when he said 'I would have clattered him if I'd been close enough.' Should have punched his head off. If he'd managed that he wouldn't just be one of my heroes – every England fan would worship him to this day too!

CHAPTER 9

ERIC CANTONA

Mention Eric Cantona and two things spring into many people's minds: that kung-fu kick into a coward of a fan after being sent off at Crystal Palace and his subsequent remark to the world's press: 'When the seagulls follow the trawler, it is because they think sardines will be thrown into the sea.' Spot on, big fella. I couldn't have put it better myself.

I'll get to both topics later, but first I want to talk about Eric Cantona the footballer. He was born in May 1966, something I wouldn't normally mention, only he later went on to make an advert for Nike which proclaimed: ''66 was a great year for English football – Eric was born!' Yes, I know he probably didn't come up with the slogan himself, but he was happy to go along with it, and that says quite a lot about him.

He made his debut as a professional footballer for the

French club Auxerre in 1983 but scored only twice in 13 appearances over three seasons. He was loaned to Martigues, and after his return to Auxerre he scored 21 goals over two seasons. That doesn't tell half the story, though.

I guess you could describe his period in French football as 'stormy' to say the least. In 1987, he won his first French cap, but, on the down side, he was heavily fined for punching a club-mate, his own goalkeeper, the French international Bruno Martini. In 1988, he was sold to Marseille, where he promptly received a one-year ban from the French national team for calling their coach, Henri Michel, 'one of the world's most incompetent trainers'. He was also suspended by Marseille when, after being substituted in a charity match, he kicked the ball into the crowd and threw his shirt at the referee.

Marseille then loaned him out to Montpellier where, in 1990, he was banned for ten days after smashing his boot into the face of team-mate Jean-Claude Lemoult. Marseille accepted him back before selling him to Nimes in 1991, where he received a three-match ban for throwing the ball at a referee. At the subsequent French disciplinary hearing, he walked up to every member of the panel and, one by one, called them all 'idiot' to their faces. This, not too surprisingly, earned him a further suspension and so, in December 1991, at the age of 25, he announced his retirement from football. You see, nobody understood him.

Fortunately for young Eric, he had some admirers too.

The man who was then French national coach, Michel Platini, and Gerard Houllier, who went on to manage Liverpool, were among them and they suggested he should perhaps try his luck in England. So it came to pass that in January 1992 a news agency report was titled: 'Wayward French Star to Have Trial in Sheffield'. No, it wasn't at the local Crown Court for assault, it was at Sheffield Wednesday, then managed by Trevor Francis.

The report said, in part: 'France's wayward striker Eric Cantona has been offered a chance to resurrect his soccer career at English first division Sheffield Wednesday, the club said. ... Cantona quit club soccer last month after being suspended for two months by a disciplinary commission. But Wednesday manager Trevor Francis has now offered him a week's trial, which, if successful, may lead to a permanent transfer for the French international next May. "We are still optimistic something will happen in the next couple of days," Francis said. "He was due to be here last Sunday and he has still not arrived. There are one or two technical points still to be sorted out..."

'Cantona, who has scored 12 goals in 20 games for France, said last week he would love to represent France in next June's European Championship finals in Sweden. An unorthodox character who enjoys reading Freud and painting, probably at the same time, Cantona has changed clubs five times in the last three years, usually after disagreements with coaches or officials. The president of one of his former clubs Bordeaux once described him as "mentally sick". He was also once banned from the national team for 10 months for calling former trainer Henri Michel a "shitbag".'

Eric Cantona – one of Sheffield Wednesday's All-time Greats. No, it doesn't read right, does it? It never happened, of course, and a few days later the same agency announced, not too surprisingly, 'French star walks out on Sheffield Wednesday'.

It went on to say, 'French soccer star Eric Cantona walked out on English club Sheffield Wednesday on Friday after refusing to extend his trial period into a second week. Freezing weather has restricted Cantona to just a couple of training sessions on artificial pitches during his time in England but the controversial striker declined an offer to stay longer. "I wanted Eric to stay on trial for another week in the hope the weather would improve and I could see him on grass," said Wednesday manager Trevor Francis. ... "I think that even the greatest manager in the world would not have been able to make a decision on a player after seeing him in two training sessions on an artificial pitch and one indoors. He and his lawyer told me that he is a big star in France and would lose face with the people there if he stayed for another week on trial. But I felt that after three days I couldn't make a decision and commit us to a substantial fee and wages for the loan."'

A case of 'Moi? The magnificent Eric, on trial? Vous can't do that, Trev.'

A day later he signed on loan with Leeds United until the end of that season, the last of the old First Division before the top flight became the Premier League.

Cantona's debut can't have been the most inspiring in the world: he came on as substitute for Steve Hodge in a Leeds team that managed to lose 2–0 to Oldham.

His next appearance was for the French national side at Wembley when Platini showed his faith in him by selecting him to face an England side that had three new boys in it. One of them, Martin Keown, did a good job of keeping Cantona quiet and another debutant, a young Alan Shearer, scored in a 2–0 victory, France's first defeat in three years.

It didn't take long for Cantona to start scoring in England, however. His Elland Road debut saw him score a goal as substitute in the 2–0 victory over Luton. Leeds manager Howard Wilkinson, who had signed him up after seeing him on video, explained why he used the Frenchman so often as sub: 'If it hadn't been for injuries, Eric would have spent more time on the bench than he has since joining us. He has a lot to offer, but we have a communication problem while he learns the language. We're in the trenches and by the time you shout, "Duck!" he's dead.' Wilkinson and seeing talent, there's an anomaly.

Cantona simply said, through an interpreter, 'I find English football very fast and hard, but I'm enjoying it.'

He'd soon have a lot more to say.

By the end of April that year, Leeds and Manchester United were battling it out for the title. Even though many of his appearances were as substitute, Cantona had quickly become a favourite with the Leeds fans. The chant 'Ooh, aah, Cantona' was beginning to be heard as the Yorkshire club clinched the title, and he moved to Leeds permanently for £900,000, signing a three-year contract.

During the summer, he announced he wanted a break from international football but it didn't take him long to get into the swing of things at club level in the new season. In August, he scored two hat-tricks: one in the 4–3 defeat of Liverpool in the Charity Shield and another in a 5–0 trouncing of Tottenham Hotspur. Soon a group called Ooh La La had recorded a song called 'Ooh Ah Cantona' and there were articles appearing about him in *The Economist* magazine – not the usual place for items on footballers.

It said, 'He is a French intellectual with an interest in existentialist philosophy; a rebel, he has clashed often with authority; in his spare time he writes poetry. The latest hero of the Paris salons? No, Leeds United's centre-forward. ... The great Leeds sides of the past had been famous for their discipline and teamwork. A fancy Frenchman with intello pretensions and an attitude problem seemed unlikely to go down well. On Mr Cantona's arrival, the English newspapers christened him "Le Brat". But he has become the undisputed idol of Leeds. Everywhere he goes – on or off the field – Leeds fans serenade him with a special chant of "Ooh, Ah, Cantona". The supporters' magazine, *Marching Altogether*, has been renamed *Marchant Ensemble* in his honour.'

The article ended: It is Mr Cantona around whom a cult has formed. It has been nurtured by the fact that he speaks almost no English. While British footballers mouth clichés in post-match interviews, Mr Cantona remains necessarily silent and mysterious. The first attempt to interview him on English television went as follows:

'Interviewer: Eric, magnifique!

'Cantona: You speak French?

'Interviewer: Non.'

Can't say fairer than that, can you?

Although he'd kissed and made up with the French national side and their new boss Gerard Houllier, things weren't going too smoothly on the field for Leeds. They made an early exit from the European Cup at the hands of Rangers and the League Cup after a defeat by Watford. The Premiership results weren't too brilliant either but that didn't stop the Leeds fans from adoring Cantona.

Perhaps they saw something in him the manager didn't, because at the end of November came the startling news – Cantona had signed for Manchester United for £1.3 million. One of the ironies of the move, even ignoring the fact that Howard Wilkinson let him go in the first place, was that he wasn't United's first choice. To quote Alex Ferguson, 'Because of [Sheffield] Wednesday's refusal to let us sign David Hirst, we looked around at strikers we rated and who might be available. I tried Leeds and was delighted when they agreed to release Cantona.'

Howard Wilkinson's explanation was: 'As a result of a conversation on Wednesday afternoon, a deal was struck which from my point of view was in the best interests of all concerned. This is a move which, perhaps, gives Eric a better chance of first-team football than he would have had at Leeds. Obviously, at a club with aspirations to establish itself as one of the top names in the game, it is impossible to pick more than 11 players. Somebody is always going to be disappointed.' Typical Wilkinson. With hindsight, not the best decision ever made – just ask any Leeds fan.

Eric's views on transfers are, well, typically Cantonesque: 'Leaving a club is like leaving a woman. When you have nothing left to say, you go.'

But any way you look at it, the legend was about to begin in earnest. Although 1992 isn't exactly a million years ago, it has to be emphasised that Cantona wasn't joining an all-conquering side at Manchester United. Far from it. You had to go back to the 1966/67 season to find the last time United had won the (old) First Division, the star prize in English league football, and that was with a team including Best, Law and Charlton managed by Matt Busby. During the intervening 26 years – literally a lifetime for many fans – Liverpool had won the title an amazing 11 times, Arsenal, Leeds and Everton had all won it on three occasions and even teams such as Aston Villa, Nottingham Forest and Derby County had carried off the title.

Yet United remained one of the biggest clubs not just in British football but in the world. So the scene was set for someone like Cantona to come and strut his stuff. With his natural arrogance and his shirt-collar turned up high, he had a self-belief second to none and Old Trafford was to be the perfect stage for him. Cantona had an aura about him, as all great players do, and even the opposition fans could see it.

Being Cantona, he had to describe it in his own, unique way: 'I am in love with Manchester United. I feel it like finding a wife who has given me the perfect marriage.'

Obviously Eric's way with words was infectious, because even Alex Ferguson, hardly known for his reflections on the meaning of life, said, 'Eric is an artist, and like all artists he needs a stage. He is a man searching for his theatre, and we are providing it.'

That is part of Alex Ferguson's genius as a manager. He needed a catalyst to make United the best again and realised it could be this mercurial Frenchman.

Cantona went on to score goals, yes, but not on a massive scale. It was the other qualities that he brought with him that made him stand out: he had vision, presence, he made everyone else play better around him and he could handle any pressure situation. It was as though he was born to play at Manchester United. As Alex Ferguson put it, after landing the title: 'There's that moment, we've all experienced it, when you are fiddling with a key and someone comes along and does it for you with the first turn. That is what Cantona did for us. He unlocked the door to the championship. The man has the touch of velvet. He scores goals, creates goals, and dreams up little miracles that are simply beyond the scope and imagination of most players. He is the true theatrical performer.'

In January, United went top of the Premiership for the first time that season. The following month, Cantona returned to Elland Road and the Yorkshire fans who had adored him – some of whom were in tears when he left –

shouted, 'Judas!' as his team coach arrived at the ground. But it didn't stop the Reds from gaining the point they needed to stay at the top of the table. Eric being Eric, however, that wasn't the end of the matter. He was later fined £1,000 by the Football Association for spitting at Leeds fans when walking to the dressing room after the match – worse than kung-fuing someone in my book – though the FA spokeswoman said, 'The commission did take into consideration that he was subject to provocation prior to the incident.'

United were on a roll, however, and by Easter that first title in 26 years was within their grasp. Mark Hughes was rattling goals up front and a teenage Ryan Giggs was a revelation. Peter Schmeichel, voted the best goalkeeper in the world at the time, and Steve Bruce were superb at the back, but it was Cantona, who played the last month of the season with a strapped broken wrist, who provided that extra something special. As Bobby Charlton put it, 'Great players can be quirky. That's what makes them different. You have to put up with that because of who they are. We've done that with Eric Cantona.'

United went on to win the title by ten points from Aston Villa. In doing so, Cantona had won back-to-back titles with different clubs. People were practically queuing up to echo Bobby Charlton's comments. Paddy Crerand, like Charlton, a member of the last United side to win the title, said, 'When Eric came, I thought he was a panic buy. I was wrong. Cantona has been the brain, the greatest difference from last season when United collapsed. Alex has never made a better signing. Cantona has won them the title.'

'This is the ideal stage for Eric,' said Mark Hughes. 'He's a very emotional player, lifted by atmosphere. He's got a great rapport with the fans, they love him here and he seems to revel in the attention. His creative ability has been very significant this season. He has helped to make us more creative, less predictable. We have definitely been a better side since he arrived.'

Cantona's poor English had not been a problem, Hughes added. 'Football is an international language and we get by on a nod and a wink.'

Surprise, surprise – Leeds manager Howard Wilkinson, whose side went down the table to 17th that season, wasn't as fulsome in his praise, saying the signing by United was a gamble that had worked! 'He does what he does well, but he does it best in a winning team. People say he won us the championship last season, but I didn't play him in any of the last crucial matches.' Do I detect sour grapes?

Anyway, with a second title under his belt, what did Eric do but suggest he might not stay with United! He told the French daily newspaper *L'Equipe*, 'I would like to be a European champion with Manchester,' but added he did not know if he would be at Old Trafford for the new season. 'I don't know. I've got two months on holiday and a lot of things could happen. The sunsets are beautiful everywhere. In the Camargue, in England, in Spain… for the moment I feel really great here. If I don't feel good here tomorrow, I'll leave. But I would have to talk to the club chiefs. I still have three years of my contract to run.'

And quite rightly he refused to accept that he had been lucky with his choice of clubs: 'Listen, when I arrived here, we were sixth and a hatful of points behind. It was a real challenge. Perhaps what was missing was a piece of the puzzle, a small but indispensable piece. I'm not like Maradona who can make a team play all on his own.'

United started off the next season in blistering form, in the Premiership and in Europe. You could tell that the marriage of Cantona and United really was perfect. He even went on record as saying, 'This is the first time I really feel settled in my football life. Some teams win and they are happy but with Manchester we must win and we must play nice football. I love that. I have tried for a long time to find the level I wanted. I love to win, I love football, I love the pass, the move, the joy and I have to find that to be content. For Manchester, it is the same. We have the same vision of football and victory. If you have 11 workmen, you will never win. If you have 11 artists, you will never win. It is important that the team complements each other and we have that.

'It is not the same football we played at Leeds, which was more direct,' he added. 'At Manchester it is more pass, move. I think we are the best team in the European Cup, with Milan and Barcelona, really I do. We can beat anybody if we play with patience and if we play with what we know. We have international players here with a lot of experience and a manager who has won the European Cup Winners' Cup. After the English clubs had five years out of Europe, it was important for me to play with players who know international football, like Bryan

Robson and Paul Ince. I don't know if it's a big thing for them to play with me, but for me it's a big thing to play with them. I can play at the level I want because I play with a beautiful team.'

You can definitely say that Eric didn't talk like most footballers. There again not a lot of the lads spent their spare time as he did: shooting, painting, playing the piano and violin. He also did a bit of yoga, wrote poetry and said his heroes included The Doors' dead singer Jim Morrison, the 19th-century poet Arthur Rimbaud and Antoine de Saint Exupery, a French novelist and fighter-pilot.

The artistic inclinations didn't stop there. 'At other clubs it has been a little like playing in a little street band who play together on the corner,' he said. 'They might not play so well and I don't play so well either. But Manchester United are a symphonic orchestra, a philharmonic orchestra of players. You can't help but perform well when you have such a perfect harmony all around you. They inspire me to produce a great symphony.'

I think he meant it's easier to play with good players and a manager who wants to play proper football.

While playing for United in the early years, he lived in a semi-detached house in the Boothstown district of the city. 'It's boring to be in a big house,' he said. 'When you are four people, why would you buy a house with seven bedrooms? Why would I do that, if not to show people that I am rich? I buy a house that I need not to show people I am rich – they already know that. The man who buys the big house with all the bedrooms he doesn't need shows he's rich, but maybe he's not rich inside. For me the atmosphere inside a house is very important: everywhere I have been with my family, it has been cosy.

'When I was a footballer I never thought I was different to other people, I just had a different job. People who are successful want to show they are different, they live in the big house and try to live in another world. I want to live in the same world. I don't have the pretension to be somewhere else. If I have 11 children, I will try to get a house with ten bedrooms.' Or maybe bunk beds, Eric?

By the start of 1994, United were an amazing 16 points clear at the top of the Premiership and had suffered just one defeat in the league. Everyone had practically handed them the title as they chased a domestic treble. When one newspaper proclaimed, 'Title Almost in the Bag for Manchester United', the date was 1 January.

There was a controversial exit from the European Cup in December, however, when they were knocked out at the group stage on goal difference. The 0–0 draw against Turkish side Galatasary in September proved particularly contentious. Cantona was shown the red card at the end of the game as a fight broke out involving players, spectators and the police, and he was given a four-match ban for his trouble. He also reportedly called the referee a 'cheat', although United later said he was misquoted, and swung a punch at the Turks' reserve goalkeeper.

March 1994 really did turn out to be a bad month for Eric. First he got sent off for stamping on an opponent at bottom-of-the-table Swindon Town and a few days later two yellow cards meant he had first use of the soap in a Highbury match with Arsenal. He got a five-match ban for all that and United started dropping points in the league: if the wheels hadn't exactly come off the cart, the nuts were loose.

But, with Cantona back in action, United won the league by eight points and beat Chelsea 4–0 in the Cup Final – he scored two penalties – as they became the sixth side in history to win the double. Not surprisingly, Cantona also became the first foreign player to pick up that season's PFA Player of the Year – the award voted for by his fellow professionals.

Cantona started the following season in typical fashion: he was sent off in a pre-season friendly at Rangers for a lunge at an opponent a minute after being booked. That was nothing, though, compared to the storm that blew up after the legendary game at Crystal Palace in January. It had been a fairly ordinary night for Eric, in that after 48 minutes he was sent off for trampling on an opponent. As he headed for the tunnel, however, it all – as they say – kicked off as he passed the Crystal Palace fans.

Versions vary of what was said, but within a second he had raced to the crowd and kung-fu kicked one of the fans who'd been taunting him from behind the barrier. The fan, window-fitter Matthew Simmonds, had raced down 11 steps of what he thought was the sanctuary of the family enclosure, and says he shouted, 'Off you go, Cantona! An early shower for you!' What a load of bollocks. Others there say he said, 'You French bastard, fuck off back to France!' Simmons later admitted he may have sworn.

Either way Eric was right in the *merde* this time. United

banned him for the rest of the season and fined him £20,000. The FA banned him until the end of September and fined him £10,000. The French axed him as national team captain. He ended up in court and had to do community work. After his court appearance, he attended a press conference and came out with the immortal words, 'When the seagulls follow the trawler, it is because they think sardines will be thrown into the sea.' He then pushed back his chair and left the room. Magnifique!

Let's deal with the philosophising first. When he said that, he was obviously trying to show that he possessed a deep intellect. If an English player had said it, you'd just think he was a twat, wouldn't you? Because someone is French they could go on about 'I am the moon, the team are my stars, the fans are my universe' and just about get away with it. I think they should just stick to 'I'm over the moon' or 'I'm sick as a parrot'. Because it's coming across with a French accent it's the same as their movies where you think – It must be good because it's in French and it's in black and white – even if you don't understand it.

But as for the sending off: you have this knob who thinks that because he is in the safety of the crowd he can abuse another man who is no more than ten yards away. I am a great advocate of you pay your money to go into a football ground and you have every right to boo or sing what you like. But if you think that is going to make it better for your team – or think booing and abusing is going to put opposition players off – then you are so mistaken it is frightening. Players are so mentally strong that it's only going to make opposing players want to play better and shut you up.

Every time you watch a game on television and a player takes a corner or a throw-in, you can see the hatred on the faces of some of the fans. It comes down to a tribal thing and, because they have the safety of being in a crowd and the players can't do anything to them, they think it's all right to abuse them verbally or racially or as they choose. If you did that in any other walk of life you would be arrested. Everyone knows that, if they met the same player in a bar or in the street, they wouldn't dare say anything to them one-on-one.

Doing things in a crowd is the coward's way. I had it in my career. At Colchester when I started, it was so quiet you could hear someone open a packet of crisps, so you'd hear every remark. I'd sometimes turn round to the crowd and say, 'Who the fuck said that?' and no one would say a dickie bird. I've been booed by away fans, home fans, everyone in fact. They have a right to voice their opinion on your performance because they have paid their money, so that is fine. But there is a line to be drawn.

Obviously this bloke was giving it to Cantona and something inside of Cantona's head said, 'I'm not going to take this from this twat. Why should I?' The idiot thought he was safe, but Cantona did what every player who has taken abuse over the years has wanted to do. Instead of smashing him in the face with a right hook, he launched himself and the fear on the no-mark's face is great to look at. Was it a good example for a player to set? The answer is no. Was it wrong for a player to do it?

The answer is yes. Was it understandable? Undoubtedly. Every footballer has wanted to do something like that, 100 per cent.

After his return from exile and all those months away from the game, the Cantona myth, if anything, grew even greater. In his absence, United had narrowly failed to win the title for a third year running, finishing a point behind Blackburn. With Cantona back in their ranks, they won the title for the next two seasons. In other words, they won it in the four seasons he played continuously for them, missing out only in his ban year.

When Cantona came back in that 1995/96 season, he also scored the late winner in the Cup Final against Liverpool. Five minutes from time Liverpool failed to clear a corner and Cantona's twisting right-foot volley from the edge of the area went into the roof of the net for the only goal of the game. He was captain that day and became the first non-British or Irish player to hold the Cup aloft as skipper. As he said afterwards, 'You know that's life. Up and down.'

Eventually, he was voted Manchester United's Player of the Century on the club's official website, beating into second place his only serious rival, George Best. That shows what Alex Ferguson knew all along about Cantona. How important he was, not just in the year that he signed him but also in the development of Manchester United Football Club and of the players around him. Fergie also showed superb man-management in guiding a player who had appeared uncontrollable throughout his career, never publicly criticising him in any article.

Even Cantona makes mistakes, though. Later, he turned to acting. Footballers may think that because they perform on a 'stage' and they are in a 'theatre' they are an 'artiste' but they are not. When you are playing football you're just being yourself. Don't make yourself look a prat by trying to be someone or something else. Not that I think that would worry Cantona – he never did care what people thought of him anyway.

CHAPTER 10

RONALDINHO

I wonder if all Brazilian fathers christen their sons with a view to their becoming footballers? They all seem to be called Ronaldinho or Ronaldo or Robinho or something like that, and it can be very confusing. Aren't any of them called the equivalent of John Smith?

With Ronaldinho it's even more complicated than usual and you have to concentrate to follow this. He was actually named Ronaldo de Assis Moreira when he was born in south-east Brazil in March 1980. He came to be called Ronaldinho, meaning 'little Ronaldo', to avoid confusion with the other Brazilian striker Ronaldo, the 'fat one' as Jose Mourinho calls him. (To complicate matters further, the 'fat' Ronaldo was also called Ronaldinho at one stage, but let's not go there.)

Either way, the man who became Ronaldinho – I'm talking now about the thin one with the buck teeth who scored with a free-kick over David Seaman's head in the World Cup – was bound to be a footballer no matter what name he went under. He's the one who always plays with a smile on his face. My thinking about that is that it's an act of nature. With hamsters like he's got, you can't help but smile all the time. Inside he could be seething with rage and anger, but he has to keep on smiling – there is nothing he can do about it.

There is this theory that all Brazilians are beautiful. Perhaps Ronaldinho is 'beautiful on the inside', what you might call 'a beautiful person'. That's what God's done. He's said, 'You are going to be talented – you are going to be a great footballer. The downside is that you're going to be all that but with a face like Bugs Bunny. Oh yes, and I'm also going to give you a rascal barnet. A bit like Bob Marley meets Harpo Marx.' He could iron that all day and it would still come out like coiled springs. Despite all that, Ronaldinho hasn't done too badly. What is really annoying, although I admire him for it, is that he's had absolute darlings flocking round him for years.

His father, who had played football for a local club, worked in a shipyard and died of a heart attack when Ronaldinho was just eight years old. The family were very poor and his elder brother Roberto signed for the town club Gremio, who provided the family with a house, only for the brother's career to be cut short by injury.

The little boy was already showing exceptional skills not only at football but also as a futsal player. That's a kind of indoor football but unlike five-a-side there are no walls or boards to hit the small, less bouncy ball off. It leads to fantastic skill as the game is built around technique, ball control and passing in very tight areas. It encourages the natural skills of the players and it's popular in Brazil where there's a lack of full-size pitches for schools to play on.

Ronaldinho's first taste of football fame came at 13 when a local paper wrote about him after he'd scored every goal in his side's victory. Well, they did win 23–0. In 1997, he was a star of the World Under-17 Championship in Egypt, which Brazil won. Back home, he made his senior debut for Gremio and soon the talk about him coming to Europe began. His name was linked with Arsenal, which I can believe, and with St Mirren, which somehow doesn't sound quite right, even though it would have only been for a short spell while he waited to join Paris Saint-Germain. He joined the French club in 2001 and by all accounts he certainly took to the bright lights of Gay Paree.

The club's coach Luis Fernandez criticised him for the amount of time he spent in the city's nightclubs and really got the hump when his young star smuggled a girl back into his room at the team hotel the night before a key match. (Top man!) 'The problem with Roni is that he does not lead the lifestyle of a top sportsman,' Fernandez said. 'He has so much ability but that could be his downfall. I don't have a problem with him. He has a problem with himself. I can control what happens at the training camp, but not outside. Roni is 22 years old but he has to understand that recuperation is important when a player is physically fragile.'

Ronaldinho was reluctant to take French lessons when he arrived, but managed to pick up enough of the lingo to call Fernandez 'fils d'un putain' – son of a whore – when he was substituted in one game. In another match he refused to come off when the coach wanted him to.

On another occasion, he was allowed to go home to Brazil for Christmas on the strict instructions that he report back to PSG's training ground on 28 December. He arrived in his BMW 4x4 on 2 January, wished his team-mates Happy New Year and then went off to make a phone call. Goalkeeper Lionel Letizi insisted he join the other players in the changing room and explain his absence. He did at least come up with an interesting excuse when the club officials asked why he was late back; he told them he'd been having dental treatment! Lucky to get back before Easter then. The club fined him £1,300 and ordered him to follow a rigorous training routine separate from the rest of the team.

Ronaldinho was one of those players who was doing better for his country than for his club, although you've got to take into account the men he was alongside. He's one of the few Brazilians who have played for their country at every level. In 1999, within the space of three months, he both played for Brazil in the World Youth Championships in Nigeria and got his first full cap, against Latvia.

By the time the World Cup finals in Asia came around in the summer of 2002, he was one of the biggest names in a Brazilian side already boasting Ronaldo and Rivaldo. He scored two goals during the finals but the one everyone remembers is that long free-kick in the quarter-final against England – the one that sailed over poor David Seaman's head early in the second half.

It was a fluke, I'm sure of that. It just sliced off his boot and I don't fault Dave Seaman at all, even though the cheeky little Brazilian tried to take all the credit for it. 'My team-mate Cafu had told me that Seaman usually moves forward preparing to take the square balls. I was a bit far out but I tried it and I was able to score. He moved back but couldn't stop it. I had a shot at goal and I was lucky.' Bollocks! He shanked it.

Rio Ferdinand met him in the dope-testing room after the game and he agrees with me that it was unintentional. He says he asked him, 'Was it a cross or a shot? Did you mean that?'

Ronaldinho laughed and indicated a freak goal.

'He admitted he didn't mean to shoot,' Ferdinand said. 'When he started laughing I knew it was lucky. I don't care what anyone says, it was not meant to have been a shot.'

For once the smile was wiped off his face when he was shown a straight red card for a lunge at Danny Mills soon after the goal, although he and the rest of the Brazilians said it was unfair. 'It wasn't a red-card offence,' Ronaldinho said. 'Mills himself, who suffered the foul, told me this and everybody in the stadium saw it.'

His team-mate, ex-Middlesbrough star Juninho, added his tuppence-worth: 'He is not the sort of player who goes out to intentionally hurt somebody. The referee didn't know what sort of person he was so he sent him off. It was a mistake.'

It doesn't matter what sort of character you are – a foul's a foul.

It's a wonder that he had any energy for football, mind you, given the stories that emerged about his training. A lap-dancer he met in a Paris nightclub said he played a type of keepie-uppie with her for eight hours and was 'like a pneumatic drill'. A 23-year-old business consultant he met in Malaysia (where the squad were preparing for the finals) tried to get his autograph and ended up having a similar early-morning session. No wonder he once came second in a list of soccer playboys, behind George Best but way ahead of third-placed Sven-Goran Eriksson.

He even said, 'I know people are saying they want me to wear Beckham's number seven shirt. I know I do not have his looks but I hope my football is beautiful on the pitch and that is what I enjoy. I am like many men. I love being with women and that sometimes gets you into trouble, but I am a young person who enjoys life. But football is my focus now and I enjoy playing more than anything else, so playing for Brazil and my club will always come first.'

None of it seemed to slow him down, and, although he missed the semi-final against Turkey, he was back for the final against Germany. For once he wasn't the star of the show – a back-to-form Ronaldo (that's the 'fat one') scored twice to beat the Germans – and then he too started to go on about sex, saying it wasn't as good as the World Cup. 'Both are very hard to stay without and I am sure that sex would not be so rewarding as the World Cup. Sex, I am going to do in a few moments, but nothing can be so rewarding as the World Cup. Not that sex is not good, but, you see, a World Cup is every four years, sex is not.'

I don't know what they put in the coffee in Brazil, but I wouldn't mind some.

By this stage, Ronaldinho was dissatisfied with PSG for failing to make an impact in Europe, so it came as no surprise when he was transferred a year after the World Cup. The shock was that Manchester United, who appeared to be favourites for his signature, lost out to Barcelona's £21 million bid. Just to rub it in, he said his choice was prompted by the Spanish club's rich tradition of having great players such as Diego Maradona, Johan Cruyff and the Brazilians Romario, Ronaldo and Rivaldo on their books at one time or another. 'Many of the players who have passed through here are part of the history of football. I chose Barcelona because it has everything a player [and playboy] could wish for or need. It's a great club.'

Barcelona had been in decline for a few years. They had won La Liga six times in the 1990s, but those glory days had finished. They'd finished the previous season in sixth place and they needed a new figurehead. Thirty thousand supporters turned out to greet him and see him hold aloft the number ten shirt he would be wearing. 'There are a lot of top-quality players here and I feel privileged to be part of the Barcelona squad,' he told them.

It was at Barcelona during the next five years that he confirmed his status as a truly great player. In his first season, he scored 15 goals as Barça moved up to finish second in La Liga and in December 2004 he was named by FIFA as Best Footballer in the World. That was soon followed by another Best World Player award, this time based on the votes of 40,000 professional footballers worldwide.

Six months later, Ronaldinho helped Barcelona win La Liga 2005 easily, ahead of Real Madrid; he also picked up the Ballon D'Or for being European Footballer of the Year.

Barça won the Spanish title again the next season but more importantly they also won the Champions League after a 14-year wait. Wealthy Chelsea were beaten on the way there, and in the final in Paris they faced Arsenal. The Gunners' goalkeeper Jens Lehmann was sent off early on, but Barça still made hard work of it. Even down to ten men the Gooners could have won, but in the end that extra man told and Ronaldinho ended up being named Champions League Player of the Year.

He didn't have the greatest of games that night, but what appeals to me about him is you watch him in a game where Barcelona are struggling and he might be struggling too, yet he will do six things that stand out. He will lay a pass off with his arse or something like that, and that is what people pay to see. On the TV programme *Soccer AM* they will show ten examples of 'showboating' and six of them will be him in the same game. But he's not doing it to get on television – he's doing it to show how good he is. And it's not really showboating if it comes off, is it?

Even legends have their problems, though. After his

brilliant 2002 World Cup, the finals in Germany four years later were a disappointment for him and for Brazil, who struggled throughout and made an early exit from the competition.

The 2007/08 season for Barcelona was also disappointing and it became clear that he was not adored as he once had been. The playboy lifestyle must have been taking its toll. The answer to that was simple: it was time to move on. Eventually, he moved to AC Milan for £14 million in the summer of 2008. The massive San Siro stadium was half-filled with fans who'd turned up just to see him arrive at the club – echoes of Barcelona five years earlier – and how they roared as he put on a red-and-black striped shirt bearing the number 80 (the year of his birth) for them. I can understand why too.

I look at it like this: would I put my hands in my pockets and pay to see him? One hundred per cent I would. There's a video of him playing futsal when he was about ten. He is back-heeling goals, there are overhead kicks, everything. He was actually going past people and keeping the ball in the air while he was doing it. It is fantastic. Mind you, it's a good job he didn't try that at Cornard Dynamos in Suffolk where I played at ten – he'd have been larruped into the nearest spring onion field.

CHAPTER 11

LIAM BRADY

L iam Brady is a true Arsenal legend. He had gone to
Italy a few years before I signed for the club in
September 1986, but all the fans remembered him as one of
their all-time heroes. There were heavy restrictions on
signing foreign players in those days, so, even with their
massive spending power and fanatical fans, those big Italian
clubs had to think long and hard before they signed one.

In 1980, Juventus had the option of bringing in Liam or
the South African Jomo Sono, who was playing for
Toronto Blizzard in Canada. Tough choice, eh? With all
due respect to Mr Sono and the Blizzards – sounds like a
skiffle band, doesn't it? – I think they made the right
decision when they opted for Liam!

More to the point, I think Liam made the right choice
too. His thinking was that he wanted to challenge himself
while he was at his peak. He could never play for another

club in England – at that time anyway – so the only way he could better himself was to play for a club abroad. In his view, there was no bigger club in this country than Arsenal, so he had to go overseas. I was only a lad at the time, but I still remember what a shock it was when he left.

Liam, 'Chippy' to the fans, was born in Dublin in 1956. He signed schoolboy forms for the Gunners in 1970, turned professional at 17 and Bertie Mee gave him his debut against Birmingham soon after that. Liam is part of a long tradition of Irish guys playing for Arsenal – fitting really, given all the Irish in that part of North London. In recent years we've had David O'Leary, Frank Stapleton, Niall Quinn and Pat Rice, to name just a few.

Liam was my dad's favourite player. He idolised the fella. Brady needn't have bothered putting a boot on his right foot, but boy oh boy, what a sweet left foot he had. He could open a can of beans with it.

There is a certain quality about gifted left-footed or left-handed sportsmen. When they are among the best at their particular sport, they seem so much more graceful than the other guys around them: footballers, cricketers, tennis players, it applies to them all. Look at David Gower or John McEnroe and you'll see what I mean: it all seems so elegant and effortless, so natural. The only sport where being a leftie makes someone look cack-handed is golf. Phil Mickelson is the only left-handed golfer I can think of who is half-useful.

People might say that Liam Brady didn't have pace, but when he had the ball he slowed the game down to his own speed and, like all great players, he looked as though he had that extra second to do something – a gift that ordinary players just don't have. That's what great players do: they give themselves that extra second of time. All that tackling and stuff, the hurly-burly – you get your minions to do that and then they just give you the ball.

One of the questions you always get asked about players from another era is: 'Would they be good enough to be as successful in today's game as they were in their own time?' The answer with all the great players is yes, and Liam is a perfect example of this. Among all the other qualities, the skill and finesse that he had was a wonderful 'engine' – he could keep going and going while all the tradesmen were flagging. The best example that springs to mind was Arsenal's famous win over Manchester United in the Cup Final in 1979. It was the 'middle' game of three successive finals the Gunners appeared in, and the only one of the trio they won. The previous year, they had somehow managed to lose to the Tractor Boys from Ipswich and the year after they went one better and got turned over by Second Division West Ham.

Liam was on fire that day in 1979. He helped Brian Talbot to open the scoring and then he laid on the second for Frank Stapleton to head home, which meant that at half-time Arsenal were totally in charge. The second half was pretty uneventful and, as the score hadn't changed with five minutes left, everyone in the Arsenal part of North London was getting ready to celebrate when United's centre-half Gordon McQueen tried to ruin the party by scoring. That was bad enough, but Sammy McIlroy then immediately tiptoed his way through the

Arsenal defence and equalised. Talk about snatching defeat, or a draw, from the jaws of victory. It looked all set for extra-time and who knows what would have happened then. It was a boiling-hot May afternoon, the impetus had swung towards United and the odds were bound to favour them in the extra half-hour. Fortunately, for the Gooners anyway, Chippy had different ideas.

From the restart he got possession and moved down the left side of the pitch. Some players run in such a way you can almost see the ground shaking underneath them as they thunder along. Others manage to make it more silky and smooth. The top ones, the real class acts, you'd think they were in carpet slippers they're so light as they move over the pitch. That's the category that Liam belonged in.

He had run his socks off for nearly 90 minutes and, even though it was beach weather that afternoon, he still had the energy and determination to run straight at United. They were all over the shop as he came at them, so he slipped a ball to Graham Rix that just invited him to cross it into the area. That's exactly what he did. Gary Bailey in the United goal decided to come out and wave to someone in the crowd, Alan Sunderland – he of the famous home perm – slid in at the far post and it was 'Goodnight Vienna'. It was one of those famous victories that live on in the memory. It turned into a Cup Final that everyone remembers the final five minutes of, even though they can't recall too much about the preceding 85. Alan Sunderland did well to be in the box to meet the ball but he did even better once the goal went in; he practically burst a blood vessel with his celebrations.

Chippy was at his peak around then. He won the PFA Player of the Year award in 1979, scored with a left-foot classic in a famous 5–0 victory over Spurs at White Hart Lane in the same year, and was outstanding in a two-legged victory over Juventus in the Cup Winners' Cup, which probably sealed his move.

It's got to be said that his years at Arsenal didn't overload his mantelpiece with trophies. His time coincided with that bleak period in the club's history between the Double-winning team of Bertie Mee and Don Howe and the arrival of George Graham. Strange to think that a player of his talent at a club as big as Arsenal only picked up one medal in seven years. It wasn't Chippy's fault – his quality would have earned a place in any Arsenal team of any period. In fact, a poll of the club's supporters recently voted him the eighth-greatest player in the club's history. Thierry Henry came out tops, but the relevant point is that Liam was the highest placed of the older players – guys who played for the club before Arsene Wenger arrived. All seven above him either played under Wenger or were brought to the club by him. Chippy even came above Charlie George, which really shows how well thought of he still is.

In his time at Highbury, Liam played 307 games for the club and scored 59 goals. How many more he created no one will ever be able to say, but it was bundles. Yet those statistics don't even tell half the tale. Most of my memories of the man come from watching him on TV, because as a kid I was playing every Saturday. But even watching him on the box you could tell how he would control a game purely by his skill and class. It certainly wasn't a case of bullying the opposition; he was only about 5ft 9in and hardly muscle-bound.

He was one of that generation of footballers who played hard and partied hard, but that was because they had earned the right to. He also helped other players progress. Just look at the influence he must have had on Graham Rix who played alongside him in midfield for years and ended up winning 17 caps for England. It can't have done him any harm playing alongside a master like Liam.

Given that I rarely saw him in the flesh, you can imagine how excited I was to be one of the ball boys for the 1980 Cup Final when Arsenal played West Ham. The Gunners were firm favourites as the Hammers were in the old Second Division, but I should have guessed what was going to happen. Sure enough, Trevor Brooking came up with a headed goal – it was probably the only time he'd headed a ball in his career, let alone into the net – and West Ham ended up winning 1–0. But Brady's class stood out, especially in the second half, just as it had the year before. This time, though, it didn't do any good and soon after that he was off to Italy.

He was at his peak during his Arsenal years and it's unusual for the club to let someone go when they are at their best, but it was different with Liam. Normally fans are disgruntled when one of their favourites moves on, but it wasn't the case with him. I think in a way the Arsenal fans were pleased that their best player moved on, and were proud he did so well when he became a major success over there. He picked up a couple of championship medals with Juventus and then, after they signed a certain Michel Platini, he moved to Sampdoria, Inter Milan and finally Ascoli.

I'm glad he managed to get those Italian medals, because, as well as trophies being thin on the ground at Highbury while he was there, he never appeared in major finals for the Republic of Ireland, even though he was capped for them 72 times. He missed the European Championship finals in 1988 through suspension and injury, and didn't make it into the Irish World Cup squads for 1990 and 1994. Jack Charlton was in charge of the Irish team by then and they played route one, low-risk football, and successfully too. So putting Liam Brady into a Jack Charlton side would have been like hiring Michelangelo to paint the Forth Bridge – there wouldn't be much point, would there? Still, it's strange to think he didn't fit in, because until Roy Keane came along Brady was probably the greatest player the Republic of Ireland had ever produced.

He's got to be a great player too because he's the only 'outsider' allowed in 'my song'. In case you don't know what I'm talking about, the Arsenal fans still sing a song in my honour. Its title is 'We All Live in a Perry Groves World' and it's sung to the tune of The Beatles' 'Yellow Submarine'. It's not the most complicated of lyrics: they simply sing 'Number one is Perry Groves; number two is Perry Groves; number three is Perry Groves...' and so on. Well, I did say it wasn't too complicated! Most versions have me at every position in the side, but there's another version that includes 'number seven is Liam Brady...' If anyone is going to muscle in on my song, I'm glad it's Liam.

I was privileged to meet him – and I do mean privileged; I'm not using the word to be polite – when he eventually came back from Italy. George Graham had taken over as Arsenal manager and I was his first signing. Soon afterwards, it started to be suggested that Liam wanted to come back to England. Liam asked George if he could come and train with Arsenal. He was the wrong side of 30 by then but George was under massive pressure to bring him back. When George said yes, he could train with us at London Colney, that just fuelled the speculation.

But George had no intention of having him back in the side. He wanted his own players and his two central midfield men would have to be high-energy, high-tempo players who would be busy closing people down, denying the other team space, and Liam did not fit into that kind of role. We all thought he was a great player, including George, but he'd had his glory days at Arsenal and they weren't going to come back under George.

I took part in a couple of five-a-sides with him during the time he trained with us, and I think he was grateful to be allowed to train with Arsenal again. No one tried to kick him – he wasn't the sort of player you'd do that to; we all had too much respect for him – and even at the speed we played at he seemed to have so much time.

I'd like to say that I had happy memories of playing against him once he came back to England, but that wasn't the case. There wasn't going to be room for him in the Arsenal set-up, so in March 1987 he settled for West Ham and, a month later, football being what it is, I ended up on the opposite side to my old hero when Arsenal took their lives in their hands and headed for Upton Park. I've described in my first book the match at Upton Park where a police Alsatian leaped into the crowd to control troublemakers and was hurled back on to the pitch minus an ear – bitten off by a Hammers fan. So there was always a tasty reception guaranteed down Upton Park way and that April night was no exception, especially as Stewart Robson had joined them from Arsenal a few months earlier too, so he had something to prove as well.

We'd won the Littlewoods Cup at Wembley a week earlier by beating the favourites Liverpool, the first trophy Arsenal had lifted since that Brady-inspired Cup Final win against Manchester United eight years before, and we should have been on a roll. Let's just say, the gentleman from *The Times* described it the next day as being 'a surprisingly vibrant end-of-season derby'. Well, that's one way of putting it. Perhaps a more accurate description was that both sides went at it hammer and tongs. The fans were in the same mood and at one stage fighting in the crowd held the game up for eight minutes after it spilled on to the pitch. Both teams had to be led off before the action could get under way again.

Tony Cottee gave the Hammers an early lead after Billy Bonds, who was past 40 by then, nodded the ball down to him. Martin Hayes equalised with a twice-taken penalty after Tom McAlister had saved his first shot, but Cottee got a second and the Hammers' third came from, yes, you've guessed it, Liam Brady.

He didn't really help matters if truth be told, because, when he scored his goal, his first for West Ham, he ran across to the area of the crowd where all the fun and games had been to celebrate in front of them. The referee, Dennis Hedges, booked him and said, 'Going over to that area of the crowd after the trouble that the police had had was absolutely stupid. I had to caution him because his action might have incited the crowd in the circumstances.'

Liam said the ref told him, 'We don't do that sort of thing in this country.' As he put it, 'I just wanted to celebrate my first goal for West Ham. The fact that it was against Arsenal was not important. I was just delighted to show them that the old left foot was still working.'

I was just delighted to get out of there in one piece.

The start of the following season saw Liam's 'homecoming' when he came back to Highbury with the Hammers. They lost to a goal from Kenny Sansom, of all people, late in the match. Liam admitted to a rare bout of nerves when he said, 'It's the first time this has ever happened to me. For some reason I was never able to settle down.' But you could tell he knew that times had moved on when he added, 'The Arsenal team I played in would never have played like that, but football has changed. This team hardly ever passed the ball in midfield, except to give it to Steve Williams to play long.' But he had to admit: 'They're getting as many good results as the old Arsenal side.' A lot better, methinks.

Liam was a West Ham player for the rest of his career and that involved playing in two ultra-competitive FA Cup third-round matches against the Gunners in January 1989. In the first meeting at Upton Park, the Hammers were 2–0 ahead in no time but Paul Merson grabbed a couple, which meant we took them back to our place for a replay four days later. This should have been no problem. Arsenal were top of the league, while West Ham were bottom and 26 points behind us. Sure enough, they nicked it 1–0 with a goal by Leroy Rosenior. Leroy was born in Clapham and played for England schoolboys, but won his one international cap for Sierra Leone. I wished he'd been in Sierra Leone that night when he headed the only goal of the game 13 minutes from time. George Graham was not well pleased.

Still, that defeat in the Cup meant we could concentrate on the league, I suppose, and a month later we beat the Hammers 2–1 at Highbury. I got mentioned, after a fashion, in dispatches in that game, although not quite in the way I would have liked. One newspaper said Mark Ward of West Ham and I battled it out for miss of the match. Brian Glanville of the *Sunday Times* described it this way: 'Ward, with only Lukic to beat, incredibly rolled his shot wide, and just before half-time Groves had been as inept after McKnight had thrown himself at a low cross from Dixon and lost it.' Charming.

At least I had the last laugh, ending up on the winning side and actually scoring the opening goal with a looping header over their keeper Allen McKnight. Their centre-half Gary Strodder fell down the slope on the goal-line at the North Bank end when he tried to jump to clear it. Local knowledge, you see.

While we went on to win the title that year in that famous last game of the season at Liverpool, Chippy and his new mates at West Ham didn't do as well. In fact, they were relegated. A year later, at 34, he called it a day, his last game being the final day of the season, when the Hammers beat Wolves 4–0. Like all of us, he'd had to decide it was time to bow out.

Before that match, he said, 'It will be very sad but I know within myself that this is the right time to go. I don't intend to stop playing altogether but I won't be playing professionally again – it will only be for fun. The game's a lot faster, a lot more physical and there's less of the skill element. Even those people with skill have less time on the ball. Those who influence the game want to make it more exciting by making it more direct, but is it really what fans want?'

Liam is a very thoughtful guy, just the sort of guy who should be in charge of the football academy for youngsters at Arsenal. His role as I write this is the club's Head of Youth Development, and he's perfectly suited for it. He has seen it all and done it all. He came over from Ireland as a young lad, so he has seen all the pitfalls that a young player can be caught by. He would immediately let people know what a privilege it is to play for a club as big as Arsenal without ever going down the road of saying what a great player he was when he was there. That's not his style anyway.

When the Irish made Giovanni Trapattoni their manager in 2008, one of the first things he did was appoint Liam as one of his assistants. Chippy, who played for him at Juventus, is a fluent Italian speaker. He never got to the World Cup finals as a player, which was a travesty, but you never know how it might end off the field.

CHAPTER 12

TONY CURRIE

I first remember watching Tony Currie play when I saw him on *Match of the Day*. I was probably about seven or eight at the time. It was the days of long, shaggy hair – if not that, then perhaps a perm – and he had this mass of rock-star blond barnet down to his shoulders. It was a time when shirts could be worn outside shorts and players would have their socks around their ankles if they felt like it. But he didn't just look the part, he could play as well. He also wore the number ten shirt and in my eyes that has always meant you had to be someone special.

Tony was born in 1950 in Edgware, North London, and was one of those players who you could see was the business at a very early age. As a lad he was with Queens Park Rangers and Chelsea, but he moved to Watford as an apprentice and made his debut for them when he was just 17. One of my big mates Micky Packer was at

Watford with Tony and tells me it was obvious he was going places. He scored nine goals in just 18 first-team games, not bad for a teenager playing midfield, and signed for Sheffield United when he was a month past his 18th birthday. The fee was £26,500, just about enough to cover the annual insurance premium on a Baby Bentley for one of today's superstars, but a lot for a club like the Blades to splash out back in the 1960s, especially on such a young player. It was also unusual at that time for southern lads, especially as young as he was, to head north to make their name; usually it was the other way around.

None of that held him back, though, and he went on to become a legend at Sheffield, perhaps the greatest player they ever had. But the thing that stands out in my memory all these years on is that he was the first player I ever saw who could do a step-over. For the uninitiated, that is when you roll the outside of your foot over the inside of the ball and then over the top of it, making the defender think you are going to take the ball one way so he moves his bodyweight to block you. Then, with your other foot, you take it in the opposite direction. It was a revelation to me to see this happening – and in the First Division against good defenders too.

The thing was, it's difficult enough to do slowly, but Currie was doing it at pace. Ronaldo of Manchester United does the same thing now. In fact, he can do four or five on the spin – and trust me, that's knackering – but Currie was the first I ever saw. Some people might think that it would be easy for a defender to read what was happening, but if it's done at speed it only needs the defender to shift his weight the wrong way for a second and the attacking player is away. Currie was so well balanced that he was like a ballerina – a pretty big one, sure – and he would just skip away while nine times out of ten the defender was falling on his arse. It also looked as if there was a grin on his face as he was doing it.

So there I'd be the next morning, after watching him on *Match of the Day* on Saturday night, a little kid out on the green practising by myself, trying to be just like Tony Currie. I would try to execute the trick but end up block-tackling myself, although eventually I did master it – after a fashion.

Tony Currie was the kind of player I wanted to be, an inside forward, the playmakers of their day, the entertainer. In fact, apart from him being slim, lithe and good-looking, having flowing blond hair and being able to kick with both feet, and me being a short, squat, freckled ginger who was predominantly right-footed, it would be hard to tell us apart.

Years later when I went to Arsenal, I saw that David Rocastle could do a step-over like Tony. Rocky had fantastic skill, and he could do it all the time. I could manage it in training, but I never tried it in a game at Arsenal. Our manager George Graham said to me that if he ever saw me trying a show-pony trick like that it would be the shepherd's crook for me straight away. He'd say, 'Grovesy, just stick to basics. Knock it out of your feet and go. You don't need any subtlety.' And let's be honest, it would have been more Edwina Currie than Tony Currie anyway.

Tony was playing at the same time as a great group of English flair players – Rodney Marsh, Stan Bowles, Frank Worthington – all wonderful to watch and their fans idolised them. Even all these years later, the supporters at the clubs they played for remember the type of football they played. Every side seemed to have a player like that. We didn't know it then but in its own way it was a golden age. It was all in the wake of George Best's arrival on the scene in the 1960s, when footballers started to be treated like pop stars with the photo shoots, the clothes and the birds.

Currie's time at Sheffield United coincided with their having one of the best sides they ever had. 'Coincided' is probably the wrong word, mind, as he was the main reason it was such a good side. They came up from the old Second Division and did really well for a few years. Their captain was a full-back called Len Badger and on the right wing they had a guy called Alan Woodward, who played for them for years and scored a hatful of goals. For a brief spell, they were right up with the top clubs, but it didn't last and when they were relegated Currie went to Leeds United.

Don Revie had left Leeds a couple of years earlier and they were coming out of what you might call their 'war of attrition' phase by then. Tony turned it on for Leeds just as he had at Sheffield, although he was only there a couple of seasons.

He was so good you had to put him in the England team – it was criminal to leave him out. The tragedy is that he never got a decent run in the side. He won just 17

LiThe thoughts of David Seaman: 'Oh, bollocks.'

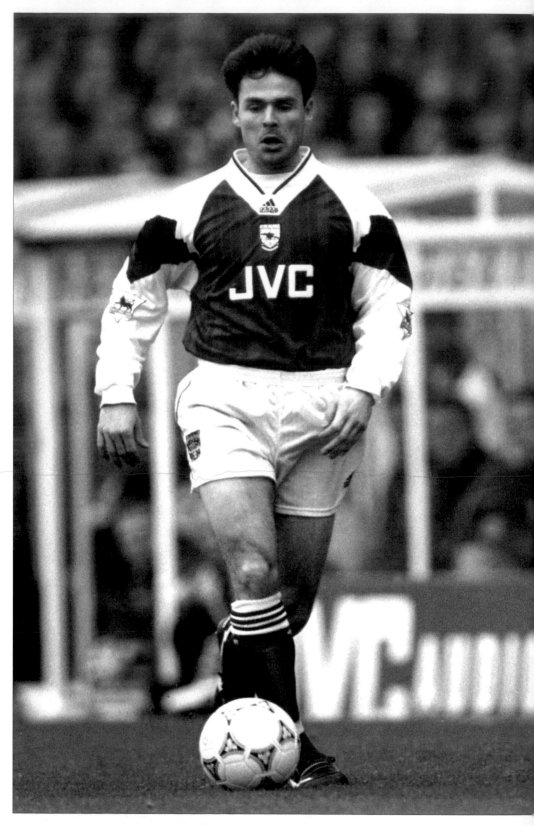

Anders Limpar showing great ball control – and with his feet too.

Mario Kempes. Head and shoulders above the rest, World Cup Final, 1978.

'Tony Currie – Curling Tongs 'R' Us?'

caps and those were spread out over seven years. It was like all those other gifted players of the time: they got a reputation as being guys you can't 'trust' if the going got tough. It was all rubbish, of course, but that's the way it was, and it can't have helped that around that time England could call on players like Colin Bell, Alan Hudson, Trevor Brooking, Ray Wilkins and Martin Peters for the midfield. But he should have been in the England team for four or five seasons.

After his spell at Leeds he moved back south and played for Queens Park Rangers before ending up at Torquay United for half a season in 1984, and that's when our paths finally crossed. They were in the old Fourth Division and he was the old 'seasoned pro' there. I was an up-and-coming youngster at Colchester, and when I read that he'd been signed by Torquay manager Dave Webb I immediately looked at the fixture list to see when Colchester were playing them.

It was a Saturday fixture at our Layer Road ground and I just hoped that he would be in their side. We were out on the pitch early warming up and I kept looking over my shoulder to see if he would be coming out too, which would mean he was playing. After a while, the great man made an appearance. He obviously liked a buffet as when he came out of the dressing room it was more of a waddle than a run, but I didn't care. I was still thrilled to be on the same pitch as him. But I also didn't want him to look too embarrassing, as the old Fourth Division was a bit muck and nettles.

I was on the right, all energy and ambition, he was

centre-midfield, all 'been there, done that'. Needless to say, he completely ran the game without even breaking sweat. Our players tried to hustle him, close him down, boot him, everything they could think of, but it made no difference. It looked as though he was in slow motion: he just glided around them and they couldn't get near to him. It was obvious to everyone that he was just different class.

One thing happened in that game that still sticks in my memory. We played a long ball over the top of their defence and for some reason he was their last man – perhaps he just hadn't been arsed to get back up field after defending a corner. The ball came to him, and me and Tony Adcock went to close him down in the corner. We thought, We've got him – the old bastard ain't going to get out of there. But he dropped his shoulder as if to give the ball back to the keeper, dummied Tony Adcock and that was Tony done for. I was the next one to engage him and I thought, I've got him now – he's got no chance.

For all those years I'd seen him do the step-overs, I'd wondered how dopey could those defenders be, because it was obvious what would happen. Then it all went into slow motion. He put his left foot around the ball and did it. I moved to the right and the whole stand on that side of the pitch swayed to the right too. We all moved in synch and dropped our right shoulders. At exactly the same moment, he skipped away to his right. I just saw this gliding figure ghost past me, exactly as it had been on the television all those years before. All right, it was probably the 5,000th time he'd done it, but as he moved away I just started clapping. He was one of my heroes and now I had been officially 'Curried'. How proud I was.

It was March or April so the grass was thin and there were bare patches down the middle and in the goalmouths. It didn't make any difference to him. He could have played on corrugated iron and his touch would have been fantastic. I never even got a tackle in on him. I could have chased after him and caught him to try to get a tackle in, but I didn't want to. I didn't want to dispel the myth.

As well as his step-overs, Currie was also a ground-breaker in another area of football. He was one of the first football stars to become a gay pin-up. Before I go any further, I must point out that, as well as liking a sherbet, he had no 'iron' tendencies, yet he ended up on the cover of a gay magazine.

I only became aware of it later on, as at the time it happened I was only ten, for God's sake, and had no idea what that kind of stuff was all about. It was at Bramall Lane in 1975 when Sheffield United played Leicester City. Leicester had a top side at that time too and one of their key players was Alan Birchenall, a good forward who'd been at Chelsea and Crystal Palace. Like Tony Currie, he had long blond hair and looked as though he spent a couple of hours before every game at the hairdressers.

Anyway, the two, who were mates, collided in the penalty area and ended up in a heap. Birchenall jokingly said to Currie, as you do, 'Give us a kiss.' So Currie gave him one. I mean, what else could a geezer do? But the exact moment their lips met a cameraman snapped the picture and the next day it was all over the papers. Soon it went around the world and was one of the most reproduced sports shots ever. It featured on main news bulletins and a question was even asked in the House of Commons along the lines of 'What is sport coming to?' Right-wing groups said that when they came to power they'd shoot them and a German gay magazine even wanted them to write a column for it. They were even asked to repeat the kiss for a photo-shoot – in bed together. They said no. Obviously not enough dough!

It was all, as they say, in the best possible taste, but I still think I prefer to remember Tony Currie for his step-overs and his other skills on the field, rather than his smooching with Alan Birchenall.

CHAPTER 13

DAVID SEAMAN

I'll never forget the first time I encountered David Seaman. He ended up picking the ball out of the net after I'd scored one of the best goals of my career. It was a bit like John Barnes's famous goal for England against Brazil. You know, the one where he received the ball on his chest on the left wing, cut inside, beat five or six defenders, glided past the goalkeeper and flicked it into the net, all in one movement.

Well, mine was exactly like that. The only difference was that his was scored against the most powerful footballing nation in the world at Rio de Janeiro's gigantic Maracan Stadium with millions more watching on television, while mine was scored for Colchester United against Peterborough at Layer Road in front of an end-of-season crowd that might just have topped 2,000.

Still, we're splitting hairs. The goal was just as good

155

and it was in a local derby too. I know Peterborough isn't all that close to Colchester, but we played so few teams from nearby that it could be classified as a derby as far as I was concerned. Forget the Milan derbies or the Old Firm rivalry in Glasgow, this was the big one. There was a feverish excitement among the crowd as I picked up the ball in midfield, raced past five defenders leaving them stranded in my wake, and found myself in the penalty area with only a green-clad goalkeeper to beat.

Suddenly it was like being face to face with the Jolly Green Giant in his little brother's goalkeeping kit. This big, imposing figure came out to meet me and there he was, a very young David Seaman, complete with his little Charlie Chaplin moustache. It was him or me. In his later years, he would stand up as long as he could when he was in a one-on-one, but in those days he went down and stretched to get the ball and I stretched too. I got there before him and it was in the back of the net. The crowd of 2,014 or thereabouts went crazy. We ended up winning 3–1 but I reckon that my goal should have counted as double when I consider the goalkeeper I put it past.

He didn't pull off any fantastic saves during that game, but even then you could tell he was a class act. He was 6ft 4in tall and he probably put an extra stone on in later years to make him look even more formidable. Down the line, when we both played at Arsenal, I would remind him about that goal from time to time. I didn't mention it too often, though – only about every half-hour.

'H', as we called him at Arsenal (short for 'Harry the Head' because his head was massive), was from

Rotherham in Yorkshire. As a youngster he was with his favourite team, Leeds United, but for some reason they decided to let him go and that's how he ended up at Peterborough for the princely sum of £4,000. He was with the 'Posh' for two years before going up in the world with a £100,000 transfer to Birmingham City in the old Second Division. He helped get them promoted but they only lasted a year in the top flight and then he was off again. He was 22 by now and one of the most highly rated young keepers around with ten Under-21 caps to his name, so Queens Park Rangers forked out £225,000 for him in 1988.

It was at QPR that he really made his name, and he got his first full cap in November that year. It was hardly the most famous day in the history of the England football team. The England side had jetted out by Concorde for a friendly against Saudi Arabia but that was probably the most exciting part of the trip, as they only managed a draw thanks to a second-half equaliser from Tony Adams.

QPR were a First Division side at the time, which meant they would play Arsenal, so our paths crossed again. For some reason, QPR always gave us trouble at Highbury – it was always difficult to score against them. It was during this period that, as well as a terrific goalkeeper, they had in defence Paul Parker, who went on to play for England in the 1990 World Cup, Danny Maddix, Alan McDonald and Ian Dawes. It was a good back-line and the real pain in the arse was that their two centre-halves would man-mark you – it was like having a second skin. It seemed as if most of the games ended 0–0.

By this time, 'H' had put on that extra stone. It wasn't like a 'Jan Molby stone' either – all around his hips and arse – it was power in the right places. It was while he was at QPR that you really began to notice how physically imposing he had become. The theory had always been that, if you were really big and carried a fair bit of weight, you would not be agile enough to move around the goal and react quickly enough. There were even quite a few 'small' goalkeepers around in those days, guys like Ipswich's Paul Cooper and Laurie Sivell. Even another of my heroes, Peter Shilton, although a big guy himself and over 6ft tall, would have been dwarfed by Seaman.

Modern-day diets, equipment, training regimes and agility exercises have helped make those big guys more supple, but at that time the Arsenal goalkeeping coach Bob Wilson would take 'H' and the other keepers for their own specialised training. It wasn't just a case of dealing with crosses and shots: he would work on their agility, rolling and diving and then recovering quickly. That recovery work was really important, because a lot of goals are scored when the keeper has parried the ball away but can't get back up and across his goal to make a second save. So they would work on transferring body weight so that, once they had made the initial save, they had to see how quickly they could regain their balance and get ready to react again.

At Arsenal they would put traffic cones in front of the keepers so that if there was a shot they had to take into account the cones in front of them or be prepared for deflections, just as the ball can take a touch off a player in a crowded penalty area during a match. Bob would do a lot of the shooting himself, but he liked it if the other players helped, especially the forwards. The reason was that forwards tend to hit the ball earlier than the rest and it provides a more realistic training workout for a keeper. He'd also ask us why we shot for the areas that we did, so that it would help his keepers to think like forwards do.

Bob also knew that, as forwards, even in a training session, you wanted to beat the goalie – it meant more to you. After he'd finished his sessions with Bob, 'H' would come over to join us and we'd try to bend the ball past him, or smash it through him. If we beat him, we'd say, 'Is anybody there?' in the way a clairvoyant would, or 'Phone call for Mr Seaman' to take the piss. Then he'd say something like, 'That's it. For the next half-hour, you lot have got no chance,' which meant we had to beat him from outside the area or the edge of the box at the closest. Nobody would score and that's when you really realised that you were in the company of greatness.

If it was working on his agility, then people would shoot at him in quick succession, but for the longer-range shots you would have to wait until he had got his positioning right. Not that I did – I'd wait until he was in one corner or on the floor and then try to smash it in. It was still good to put one past him.

'H' didn't have it easy when he joined Arsenal, as he was replacing John Lukic. It wasn't as though John had been having a nightmare. He had been very consistent, he'd helped us win the league title a couple of years earlier and he was one of the top four or five goalkeepers in the First Division. To top it all, he was very popular with the fans. There was a lot of talk about the move to Arsenal from QPR and before it actually happened the Gooners fans would chant, 'We all agree, Lukic is better than Seaman.' Even the manager who signed him, George Graham, said, 'I still think John Lukic is one of the top three keepers in the country. I just think David Seaman is the best.'

So 'H' had a lot to prove when he turned up, especially as he cost a record fee for a goalkeeper of £1.3 million. But he treated it just as he treated everything else: he simply took it in his stride. Fortunately, John Lukic very quickly moved to Leeds so there was no embarrassing crossover period. Although there is a Goalkeepers' Union where numbers one, two and three all help each other, they are only human. I'm not talking about 'H' and John Lukic here, but generally speaking they are very supportive of each other while hoping that the manager's first choice isn't going to keep on playing a blinder, otherwise they are never going to get a game, are they? They're hoping the number one will let the ball through his legs and, although they might publicly say, 'It's one of those things that can happen to anybody,' they are really thinking, Great – I might get a chance now!

The obvious exception to this was Jens Lehmann, the Mad German as he was called, when he was at Arsenal. When the team went through a bad spell, he would say the reason was because he wasn't in goal. Not only did he reckon he was better than his replacement Manuel

Almunia, he actually said so quite publicly. He also reckoned he was the best goalkeeper in Germany and that he should have been selected ahead of Oliver Kahn. Given that Kahn is generally thought to be one of the best goalkeepers of all time, has won virtually every honour going, is the only goalkeeper ever to be voted the player of the tournament in a World Cup finals (2002) and is a national institution in Germany, that shows the high opinion that Jens had of himself.

There was no pretence about Jens: he just reckoned he was the best. He had to be opinionated and good in order to follow 'H' who had become an Arsenal legend by the time he left. Incidentally, Lehmann – who was in goal in every game of Arsenal's unbeaten 2003/04 season – was really liked by all the players, management and staff for being a really down-to-earth guy. It was just when the whistle went for the game to start that he turned into a lunatic!

He was completely different from 'H' but Dave had a massive presence too, in a very different way. From the first game he played for Arsenal you could tell that he had that air about him, the way he dominated the box and came for crosses. He was totally different from the other goalkeeper I admired, Peter Shilton, in that he never blamed anyone if things went wrong. He never gave anyone a bollocking. He was not a ranter and a raver. I'm not just talking about the gestures that you could see from the back of the stand – even close-to he wouldn't have a go at anyone.

His communication was brilliant, always telling his

defenders who to pick up and who to watch out for. People talk about goalkeepers being mad, but his strength was that he was so laidback and calm. That calmness transferred itself into an air of authority and that reached the back four, who would think, There's nothing that's going to ruffle us – we're going to be all right as long as 'H' is behind us. And if he made a great save, he just used to laugh – he would smile as he got up.

One of the early games that showed his brilliance was at White Hart Lane in January 1991. The teams had already had a goalless draw at Highbury at the start of the season and by the time the return game came he'd still only let in ten league goals. Spurs were in their pomp with Gary Lineker and Gazza both playing and, to be honest, Tottenham fairly battered us. 'H' was an absolute colossus that day, clutching the ball every time they threw it into the box, collecting it on the edge of his area, making flying saves, winning the one-on-ones. The longer the game went on, it didn't seem as if he was 6ft 4in tall, it was more like 8ft 4in. I think he probably saved a kid from a burning stand and then put out the fire as well that afternoon – he was just superb. If the game had gone on much longer, he probably would have discovered a cure for cancer. No disrespect to John Lukic, but that's when you realised that, although he was a really good goalkeeper, 'H' was a great one.

Terry Venables was in charge of Spurs that day and he said, 'I don't think I've seen so many chances created against Arsenal for a long time. We should have had four or five goals but their goalkeeper was superb.'

George Graham just said, 'If you pay for the best, you get the best.'

At the end of the season, we won the title by seven points, despite having two deducted for a brawl with Manchester United, and had conceded just 18 goals in the process. The legend of the Arsenal back four was growing and 'H' and the back four didn't miss a league game. (Apart from Tony Adams and he had a good excuse: he was behind bars for drink-driving for a spell.)

'H' is like virtually every other goalkeeper on the planet, however – it's his mistakes that tend to live in the memory. Great goalscorers miss sitters and they are soon forgotten and midfield players sometimes have matches where they can't pass water. But keepers... In 1994, for example, he'd helped Arsenal win the Cup Winners' Cup, beating Parma 1–0 despite having to field a weakened side – only for the following year to bring the first of his memorable 'misses'.

Arsenal and Real Zaragoza were drawing 1–1 in the last minute of extra-time of the final of the same tournament in Paris. The ball was bouncing around in the Arsenal half and Tony Adams headed it forward only for Nayim, the ex-Spurs player, to control it. He was near the right touchline and only just in the Arsenal half. He took a quick look at goal and thought, I'll just smash it. So that's exactly what he did from a distance of over 50 yards and it ended up dipping into the net.

If you look at it now, and it pains me to say this, I do think that 'H' was at fault. It came such a long way that he took off too early and he was actually coming down as the ball went over his head. His timing was all wrong. Even Nayim said, 'My goal must have really hurt. I saw Seaman off his line and decided to have a go. It was lucky but we won and that's what counts.'

That was bad enough, but the other gigantic miss he's remembered for came on the biggest stage of all, the World Cup in 2002. England had got through a tough group that included Nigeria, Sweden and Argentina, and had then beaten Denmark to make it to the quarter-finals. The only problem was that meant they were playing Brazil, the first meeting between the two in the finals since the great 1970 match.

Everything started off fine when Michael Owen put England ahead in the 23rd minute, only for Rivaldo to equalise in injury time in the first half. A few minutes into the second half it all went pear-shaped for England in general and 'H' in particular. Ronaldinho, who was then playing for a French club before his superstardom at Barcelona, took a free-kick from around 35–40 yards out and, same old story, it sailed through the air and over Dave's head and into the far corner of the net. Again he tumbled into the netting to look like a fish in a trawlerman's catch. This time, though, I don't think he was to blame.

Ronaldinho said afterwards that he'd meant for it to happen. In my opinion, in a million years he meant it to happen. He was trying to curl the free-kick right-footed into the box, and, if you look at Dave's positioning and asked him now if he would be in the same starting position, I think he'd say yes. Some people said because of his age – 'H' was 38 by this time – he just didn't move his feet quickly enough. I don't think that's the case – it was just a fluke, a mishit that swerved and then dipped and became unstoppable. To be able to get to the ball, 'H' would have needed to be standing right by the post where it went in, which would have put him out of position.

I mentioned in my first book how he cried after a Wembley clash against Spurs because he'd let a Gary Lineker goal in and felt responsible for it and he felt to blame. Well, he was emotional after the Brazil game because England ended up losing 2–1, even though Brazil played the last 30 minutes with ten men, but I know him as a big man in every sense and he would have held his hands up if he had been to blame for the Brazilian free-kick. I have no time for footballers who cry, but his tears then weren't for himself – they were because he thought he'd let the team and country down.

He did say, 'My main thing is that I just want to say sorry to the fans,' and I'm sure he meant it, but no one should have had a go at him. I don't think he let anyone down in that game and David Beckham, who was England captain that day, summed it up right when he said, 'If anyone tries to make a scapegoat out of David Seaman I think it would be an absolute disgrace, because I think he's been the best goalkeeper in this tournament. The goal wasn't his fault. It was a fluke goal that was a cross that ended up being a goal.'

But it would be wrong to focus on the lows of a fantastic career, because he was at the top of his profession for many years. From an England point of view, one of his greatest moments came during Euro 96 at Wembley. England had struggled in drawing their first group match 1–1 against the might of Switzerland and were only leading 1–0 against Scotland when a penalty was given against Tony Adams for a challenge on Gordon Durie. Leeds' Gary McAllister smashed it to Dave's right, but he somehow got across and deflected it over the bar. It's at moments like that the goalkeeper really is a hero.

'It was the best feeling I've had in football,' 'H' said afterwards. 'I was elated when I realised the ball had ricocheted to safety… I've made some good saves in my career but this one goes right to the top. It was a crucial stage. I guessed, like I always do, and the ball hit my elbow. As McAllister ran up, the ball rolled off the spot. I thought he would stop and retake it. But he just kept coming and hit it with tremendous power. Had the ball not rolled, I would have caught it! It was a marvellous feeling to save a penalty at Wembley. Nothing like it.'

It wasn't just football fans who thought 'H' was Top Man. He made a trip to Wimbledon during the tennis tournament around that time and the crowd there forgot about the Pete Sampras game they were watching and burst into applause when he entered the Royal Box.

With all that admiration, you might excuse 'H' if he went out and had a few sherbets to celebrate. But he wasn't that kind. We had the legendary Tuesday Club for drinkers at Arsenal and, although he would join us for short spells, he never let it go too far. At the time he was married to his first wife Sandra, and he'd tell her that he was going night-fishing some Tuesdays. Most footballers play golf to get away from the missus, but it's extraordinary the lengths some others will go to! Anyway, he would set his rods and his tent up near Waltham Abbey and then come and see us for a couple of hours, have a few drinks and then go back to the riverbank. He liked to come out with the Tuesday Club as he enjoyed being with the lads and all the banter, but he wasn't one to stay all night.

I would say to him, 'Why don't you just stay in a hotel?' and he would say, 'No, Grovesy, I'm night fishing' – fishing was his big hobby, after all. I asked him if he stayed up all night fishing and he said he didn't – he'd put an alarm on the edge of the float and then have a kip in the tent, and if he got a bite the alarm would go off.

'That's not night fishing, that's alarm fishing,' I said. 'Why not pay someone to go fishing for you and, when they get a bite, they can phone you up and you come and land it? It's the same thing.'

He just shook his head and gave me a playful punch – it gave me a dead arm for days.

Later in his career, he adopted a 'Spanish waiter' look of 'tache and ponytail. I've nothing against ponytails, as long as they are on Barbie dolls, but I'm not too sure on footballers. If he'd had one when I was at Arsenal, we'd have held him down and cut it off and pinned it on Tony Adams – pin the tail on the donkey! – assuming there were enough of us brave and stupid enough to try it.

The ponytail didn't seem to slow him down when he played for Arsenal at the age of 39 in the FA Cup semi-final against Sheffield United in April 2003, his 1,000th professional game. Arsenal were ahead by Freddie Ljungberg's 34th-minute goal when, with just six minutes left, the ball was bouncing all around the Arsenal area with the defence nowhere in sight. Paul Peschisolido was so close to the goal he could almost have blown the ball over the line when he headed it to the right and past 'H'.

There was nothing wrong with the header – apart from the fact that 'H' reached it, diving backwards and to his right to claw it clear. It wasn't just a tap either: he got enough power on it to force the ball away from the danger area. It was later called one of the greatest saves of all time, ranking up there with Jim Montgomery's save for Sunderland against Leeds in the 1973 FA Cup Final and even with Gordon Banks's legendary effort against Pele in the 1970 World Cup. 'H' just said afterwards, 'I thought it was in, to be honest. I just flung my arm and tried to get something on it.'

The other members of the Goalkeepers' Union had a bit more to say. Gordon Banks himself insisted, 'You would have to put this one in the same category as mine against Pele in 1970. Pele's header came from further away than Paul Peschisolido's against David and the fact that I stopped it was probably a lot down to instinct. But the great thing with David's save is that he had his weight all on the wrong foot. He had to shift all his weight on to the other foot and then get right across his goal.

'Then he didn't just block the ball with his arm, he scooped it away, which was crucial. Had he just blocked it, the ball could well have dropped down for the Sheffield United player to knock in. For any goalkeeper, it would have been an outstanding save but at the age of 39 it is quite remarkable and so good luck to David.'

Jim Montgomery said, 'That was one of the great saves from Seaman. Coming as it did on his 1,000th appearance, it was terrific. And to have produced a save like that at this stage in his career could not have been sweeter for him, especially after people have been knocking him.'

Dave's last appearance for the Gunners was as captain of the 2003 FA Cup-winning team who beat Southampton 1–0. It was fitting that his last act for the club was to hold the trophy high above his head. He'd been first-choice goalkeeper for 13 years, won three championship medals, four FA Cup winner's medals, a League Cup and European Cup Winners' Cup medal. Soon afterwards, he left for Manchester City, but injuries affected him there and he only played a handful of games before retiring at the age of 40.

In 14 years, he also won 75 England caps, second only to Peter Shilton. Big 'H' was truly a legend among goalkeepers, yet never once did he behave like a big-time Charlie – and you can't say better than that.

CHAPTER 14

FRANZ BECKENBAUER

There are only two 'Good Germans' I can think of. One is Boris Becker. Why? Because Boris was a great sportsman, a winner, he could shag in a broom-cupboard – even if he did let the side down by only lasting for 60 seconds or so – and, above all else, he's a 'ginga' like me. The other is supermodel Claudia Schiffer. Why? You work it out.

Just behind them, though, comes Franz Beckenbauer. I classify him as an 'All Right German'. Believe me, that's pretty high as far as I'm concerned. He is certainly the best German player in history and he's probably the only man who could justifiably challenge Bobby Moore for the title of Best Defender Ever. Neither of them ever seemed to have a hair out of place or shirts hanging out of their shorts. He and Bobby could have had a turf-war for the Persil Award for the least grass stains on their kit. Yes, he was *that* good.

England has produced some great players in its time, but no one quite like 'Kaiser' Franz. The reason for that is simple: there hasn't been anyone else like him. The difference between England and Germany stood out a mile to me when I watched him and Bobby Charlton leading out their countries at Wembley in October 2000. It was the opening qualifying group match for the 2002 World Cup and the two greats were there because it was also the last game being played at the old Wembley before it was rebuilt. The pre-match build up had the lot: a version of *The Great Escape* theme tune – how very appropriate – 'Jerusalem' and then 'God Save the Queen'. The crowd booed when the German national anthem was played – what a surprise. The game ended with Germany winning 1–0 through an early Dietmar Hamann goal and Kevin Keegan resigning as England boss. All in all a pretty miserable day.

But what sticks in my mind was the difference between these two great ex-players. Beckenbauer was immaculate in his full-length, designer-label Crombie coat, razor-creased trousers and polished shoes as he strode on to the pitch. 'Immaculate' was always the word that sprang to mind whenever Beckenbauer played and he'd obviously carried it on into his later life. Bobby Charlton had on a 'Frank Spencer' raincoat that looked as though it cost £19.99 from Matalan and what seemed to be a pair of old, brown Hush Puppies. The difference between the two nations was summed up there and then.

England vs Germany has always been one of the great rivalries in football, and Beckenbauer has featured in some of the most memorable games between the two countries. Basil Fawlty may have said not to mention the war, but I will. That's the reason there is always an edge to games between the two countries, of course it is. There's an old joke about the Germans celebrating a victory over England and going on about how they'd beaten us at 'our national game'. Back comes the reply: 'Well, we beat you twice at yours – in 1918 and 1945.' We also beat them in 1966 too, but I'll get to that later.

In recent years, England vs Argentina has always been a bit tasty, made worse by the Falklands War, and England vs Scotland is traditionally a grudge match because the Scots want to be better than us but know they never will be. But England vs Germany is the big one. You see, the Germans really do believe they are better than us. And what Englishman can say, hand on heart, he feels totally confident of our chances whenever we come up against them? Beckenbauer typifies why we are so nervous about taking them on.

He was born not long after the war ended in 1945 and at the age of 17 he gave up his job as a trainee insurance salesman to become a professional footballer with Bayern Munich. Nowadays we think of Bayern as the best team in Germany but it wasn't like that when Beckenbauer joined them. They weren't even in the Bundesliga when it was formed in 1963 but they were soon promoted into it and the next year he made his first-team debut – as a left-winger. It didn't take long before he switched into midfield and his international debut came in a crucial World Cup qualifying game against Sweden. He was coolness personified in the 2–1 victory, which meant that, at the age of 20, he was about to burst on the world scene.

The place was England in 1966 and the tall, young midfield player was immediately one of the stars of the tournament. There were stars all over the place: Pele (before he was kicked off the park), Eusebio of Portugal, Uwe Seeler of West Germany, not to mention the English players. Yet Beckenbauer appeared from nowhere to rival them all.

In West Germany's first game, he glided through the Swiss defence on two occasions to score in the 5–0 rout. He then helped his side draw with Argentina and beat Spain to move through to the next round. He scored again against Uruguay in a 4–0 win and in the semi-final his stunning left-foot shot from outside the area bent around the Russian defence and left their goalkeeper, the legendary Lev Yashin, clutching the post in disbelief.

That meant they would play England in the final and we all know what happened there. What isn't so widely known is that the West German manager, Helmut Schön, made Beckenbauer mark Charlton as he was the player the Germans feared most. Schön's assistant, Dettmar Cramer, felt that asking Beckenbauer to mark Bobby Charlton would sacrifice creativity but Schön thought it worth the risk. Beckenbauer followed Charlton all around the park, a 20-year-old marking the great man in his prime, and he did a good job of it too. By his standards, Bobby Charlton had a comparatively quiet game, although Beckenbauer did have the grace to admit years later: 'England beat us in 1966 because Bobby Charlton was just a bit better than me.'

The next year, Bayern won their first European trophy, the Cup Winners' Cup, beating Rangers 1–0, and alongside Beckenbauer were names that he was to be linked with for the next ten years: goalkeeper Sepp Maier and centre-forward Gerd Muller, the man who came to be known as 'Der Bomber'. In 1968 came the West Germans' first victory over England, a 1–0 win in Hannover when the Kaiser scored the only goal, and the next year Bayern won their first Bundesliga championship.

It was in the late 1960s that Beckenbauer first started to play in the position that made him famous, attacking with great effect out of central defence. To him it seemed obvious: it was one of the best places to attack from as no one ever marked the central defender. He would just wait for the right gap to appear and he'd glide into it. Dead simple really, as long as you are good enough to do it.

It worked a treat for Bayern, although Beckenbauer would still be in midfield for the national side for several years to come. Basically, he invented the role of attacking sweeper. 'There was no change to the system itself,' Schön explained, 'but Franz's outstanding ability and exceptional football brain enabled him to launch attacks as well as cover our markers.'

Then came the game that still hurts Englishmen almost 40 years after it was played. In the 1970 World Cup in Mexico, England were ahead through goals from Alan Mullery and Martin Peters with a little over 20 minutes to go. Then Beckenbauer picked up a rebound on the edge of the area and shot from outside the box across Peter Bonetti. 'The Cat' was in goal as Gordon Banks was out with a stomach upset – probably the most famous sporting 'runs' in our history – and, although he just about got down to the shot to his right, it went under his body. Cue German comeback: Uwe Seeler equalised and in extra-time Muller got the winner. Poor old Alf Ramsey was criticised for taking Bobby Charlton and Peters off, but Beckenbauer's goal – which brought the Germans back into the game – was scored while Charlton was still on the field. Talk about snatching defeat from the jaws of victory, though.

The West Germans' subsequent semi-final against Italy is often called 'The Game of the Century' and the Italians won 4–3 in extra-time. Beckenbauer played a large portion of the game with his arm in a sling as he'd dislocated his shoulder and there were no more substitutes available. So he'd got true grit as well, and, even wearing a sling and obviously in pain, he still didn't have a hair out of place.

Soon afterwards, he became the German captain and perfected that attacking sweeper role so well he was voted European Player of the Year when they won the European Championships two years later.

In 1974, Germany hosted the World Cup with a team of stars, none of them bigger than Beckenbauer. These were the great days of the tournament and I remember being so excited as a schoolboy watching it, even though England weren't taking part. The big thing at the time was to own a pair of Adidas Beckenbauer Supers, football boots with his name on that had three stripes down the side and cost about £9.99. That just shows what an

international name he was by then – selling football boots
to English kids even though he was a German!

The West Germans went on to win the tournament,
even though most people reckoned they weren't the best
team in it. That honour belonged to Holland with Johan
Cruyff but that German willpower saw them through,
even though they went behind in the final without
touching the ball. The Dutch kicked off and proceeded to
taunt the Germans by keeping possession. They strung
together 16 passes inside their own half before Cruyff
made ground and avoided the challenge of Berti Vogts
before falling under Uli Hoeness's clumsy tackle inside the
penalty area.

The referee Jack Taylor was a Wolverhampton butcher,
the type of referee you don't see any more. He had
Brylcreemed black hair that looked as though it had been
cut by an army barber and he wore baggy black shorts.
He immediately blew and pointed to the spot. It was the
first penalty ever given in the final of a World Cup and,
as the German crowd went silent, Beckenbauer said to
him, 'You're an Englishman.'

I met Jack when I was a youngster at Wolves a few
years later and he was a good bloke. What balls he must
have had to give a penalty so early in the game in front of
the German home crowd. He just walked away from all
the German players with that 'We won the war – fuck off'
air about him. Later on, he awarded a penalty to the
Germans, although he gets angry if anyone suggests that
it was to even things up, and Muller eventually scored the
German winner.

I've got to say that game showed the qualities I admire in German football. I like their self-belief and the fact that even when they are behind you can never write them off. I wouldn't pay to see most of them play, but they do carry out their jobs to the letter. They have had a lot of great players in their time, but not many of them had any flair. There's Beckenbauer himself, of course, and in the 1970s they had Gunther Netzer, but it is their mental strength that has made them a strong football nation. They never crack under pressure. Just look at them when it comes to penalties: you just know they're going to score every time.

In 2002, they took what everyone back home was calling 'the worst German team ever' to the World Cup finals and somehow got through to the final itself. It might not have been a brilliant team, but it was a great achievement that owed everything to their character.

The 1970s were a time of astonishing success for the Kaiser. As well as West Germany's victories, Bayern Munich, who provided the core of the national side, became the best team in Europe a mere decade after getting into the German top division. With Beckenbauer as captain, they won three successive Bundesliga championships and three successive European Cups – thrashing Atletico Madrid 4–0 in 1974 after a 1–1 draw, conquering Don Revie's Leeds United 2–0 in 1975 and beating St-Etienne of France 1–0 in 1976. They also won the World Clubs Cup in 1976 with a 2–0 aggregate victory over South American champions Cruzeiro of Brazil. They were, undoubtedly, the premier club side not just in Europe but also in the world. In 1976,

Beckenbauer was voted European Footballer of the Year for the second time, even though West Germany lost that year's European Championship final to Czechoslovakia in a penalty shoot-out.

The Kaiser had won a record 103 caps for West Germany when, in 1977, he accepted a $2.5 million contract to play for the New York Cosmos in the North American Soccer League. He stayed for four years, during which the Cosmos won the Soccer Bowl three times. He then returned to play in Germany, where he helped Hamburg win the Bundesliga, before opting for one final season with the New York Cosmos before retiring in 1984. And, of course, a lot of great European footballers, and some not-so-great ones, earned a final payday in America at that time and I don't blame them one little bit.

No sooner had Beckenbauer retired as a player than he was appointed as West German national manager succeeding Jupp Derwall, even though he had no coaching experience at all. You can't expect a little thing like that to hold a man like Beckenbauer back. Somehow he managed to take a pretty uninspiring German side to the final of the 1986 World Cup, where they lost to Maradona and his Argentinean mates, and four years later he took them all the way in Italia 90. This time they beat Argentina: it was a dreary match, but it meant that Beckenbauer became the first man to win a World Cup both as captain and as coach.

He then moved into club management at Olympique Marseille before returning to Bayern as coach in 1994, guiding them to the Bundesliga title and then moving upstairs as the club president. He's since become one of the big movers and shakers on the world football scene, and played a key role in ensuring Germany hosted the 2006 World Cup. Even the German Chancellor Angela Merkel said he was the man who swung it for them. He is always in the VIP box at every major game involving the German side. Whenever his picture appears in German newspapers, there is no description of his job in football or mention of his past record. Everyone knows him so well that there is no need.

Given that he appears to be Mr Perfect, it's reassuring to know that he isn't quite as dull as German dishwater. There's no point in looking like a male model and not using those looks, is there? He's been married three times, has five children – the first when he was 17 – and fathered one child after a fling at Bayern Munich's Christmas party with a young secretary at the club. He said it 'wasn't a great crime' and that he was thrilled at being a father again in his late fifties! 'I mean, imagine it, me, a father again at my age. Who would have believed it? I didn't think that life still had such a surprise in store for me.' Beckenbauer, a granddad by this time, even added, 'The Dear Lord rejoices over every child.' Sod the maintenance lawyers. Top man – ten out of ten for him there then.

Other eyebrow-raising events in Beckenbauer's life include choosing to live in Austria with its lower taxation – he simply ignored the criticism that brought on his head. More questionable was that he later had a go at German coach Jurgen Klinsmann for living in California while in charge of the national side.

As President of Bayern, he fined captain Oliver Kahn £15,000 and banned him for a game for leaving the team's Christmas party early. The Kaiser said that as club captain Kahn should have set a better example and stayed. 'It's a time that brings the team together,' he said. 'He's the captain and he just gets up and leaves early.'

Another time, after English fans had run riot in Europe, he said he wished they'd go back to their 'overcrowded island'. Can't say I blame him for that – I'd feel the same if I were German.

As his old Bayern and West Germany team-mate Paul Breitner said of him, 'He did everything that a German is not supposed to do. He got divorced, he left his children, he eloped, he had tax debts, he left his girlfriend.'

No matter what he's done off the field, it's what he did during his playing career that makes him a legend as far as I'm concerned. He was a German who had all the qualities we know and hate – sorry, should that be love? – about them as a nation, but then he added his own star quality.

That's why, bearing the war in mind, it's always somehow twice as good when England beat them as it is when we defeat other countries. That 1–0 defeat at the old Wembley in October 2000 was a disaster, but England were to surprise everyone in the return match in Munich, of all places. Even though they went behind very early on, they ended up 5–1 winners, helped by a Michael Owen hat-trick. It was one of the best displays by an England side in years and the German fans were trooping out of the stadium long before the final whistle. It was a national humiliation for them – yes, it was great, wasn't it? – and their side just fell apart.

One thing's for sure: I bet the Kaiser was saying to himself, 'This wouldn't have happened in my day!'

CHAPTER 1

ALAN SHEARER

The first time I became aware of Alan Shearer was in April 1988, when he was a last-minute choice for Southampton against Arsenal at The Dell. Paul Merson, who knew him from the England Under-19 squad, gave his verdict to the rest of us shortly before the kick-off. The 17-year-old Shearer was 'not a natural goalscorer', he said. 'He runs the channels well, holds the ball up well and is quite strong. But he is not a box player.'

'That's great,' said George Graham. 'Thanks, Merse.'

It was a First Division match so obviously reports of it were in all the papers. Here's how *The Times* reported it: 'Alan Shearer, the first player in 21 years to score three goals on his full league debut – and possibly the first-ever to do so on his debut in the first division – left The Dell on Saturday clutching the match ball autographed by players who were once his heroes, after helping

Southampton hand out a 4–2 defeat of Arsenal. Shearer, aged 17, was drafted into the Southampton team three hours before kick-off and responded by scoring three times in 49 minutes. The last player to achieve the feat was Colin Viljoen, of Ipswich Town, who did so against Portsmouth in a second division match in 1967.'

Yeah, thanks, Merse.

When we reported back for training the following week I went up to Merse and said, 'The gaffer wants to see you.' He looked at me quizzically and I said, 'Steve Burtenshaw [our chief scout at the time] is leaving and with your shrewd judgement he wants you to fill the vacancy.' I added, 'Your area is Outer Mongolia.'

This player who was 'no good in the box' was to go on to become one of the greatest goalscorers of his generation, breaking records everywhere he played. He also had the finest accolade any true footballer can receive and one that makes me envious – and I'm not that sort normally. Forget all those caps and Player of the Year awards, how about this for recognition of services rendered? At St James' Park, the Newcastle United ground where he was worshipped, they named a bar after him.

If only they had done that for me at Highbury or The Emirates. I can just see it now: Groves' Bar. Yes, it definitely has a ring to it and I can guarantee the tills would never stop ringing, with my money as well as everyone else's. So what did Alan Shearer do that I didn't, apart from score 30 goals for England in 63 appearances, hold the record for goals scored in the Premiership and pick up an OBE along the way? Life's not fair.

Shearer was born in Gosforth, Newcastle-upon-Tyne in 1970, where his father was a sheet metal worker. As a teenager he joined the famous Wallsend Boys Club – who also produced such players as Peter Beardsley, Steve Bruce and Michael Carrick – and it was there he was spotted by a Southampton scout. The fact that he was prepared to go to the south coast shows he was willing to go out of his comfort zone, and it says it all about him as a person and as a man.

When I played against him, even though he was still only 18 or 19, he was what you might call an old-fashioned, man's man type of centre-forward. By that I mean he was hard, tough and put himself about. Not overly dirty but he could mix it if the situation warranted it. He didn't moan or groan either – not in the whingeing sense – he was a no-nonsense player who just scored goals. It has to be said, though, he had good technique too.

The funny thing is that after that hat-trick against Arsenal it took him quite a while to get a regular place in the Southampton side. They had Matt Le Tissier and Danny Wallace (who would later join Manchester United) up front and it was difficult for him to get in the starting line-up. But Southampton were always struggling against relegation and you just felt when he did get in the side that it was a stepping stone – it wouldn't be all that long before he moved on to bigger and better things. It seemed inevitable he would get into the England team sooner rather than later, even though he had a rascal barnet at the time – a little blond tuft and shaved at the sides.

It didn't stop him scoring on his debut, though, as

England beat France 2–0 at Wembley in February 1992 – the first defeat the French had suffered in 20 games over three years. Shearer scored with a lethal shot and he made the second for Gary Lineker. One headline read 'Shearer Sinks the French' – and that was in a French newspaper.

'It was the greatest night of my life,' he said after the French game. 'I didn't want it to end. It has all come so quickly for me. I half-wish it would slow down a bit so I can enjoy it. When I scored I couldn't wait to get my hands up in the air. I've never had a feeling like that in my life before. They talk about replacing Gary Lineker but how can you replace a player like that? No one will ever take his place in my book. I was glad I made the chance for his goal in the second half. I enjoyed playing with him, but then again I enjoyed everything about the night, playing alongside David Hirst in the first half, everything.

'Scoring against France even beats the hat-trick on my debut for Southampton and that was really special. There was a bit of pressure on me but I didn't feel it too badly, even though Gary was watching from the bench in the first half. I knew all I could do was to be myself and try my best. Now I hope that I can go back down to Southampton and help lift them away from the bottom of the table. But at the moment I just want to savour the night.'

That night, he showed all the characteristics that he displayed throughout his career. He had great pace (until knee injuries got to him) and good upper-body strength. But – and this may sound a bit stupid – his biggest strength was that he played to his strengths. By that, I mean he knew what he was about. Look at his finishing.

He wasn't one of those who tried to chip the goalkeeper or bend it into the far corner: most of his strikes were down to pace and power. Like all good headers of the ball, he was brave in the air and when it came to penalties he's one of the few English players in recent times you'd put your mortgage on to score from the spot. He just blasted it.

Our paths crossed again, after a fashion, that summer when he was transferred to Blackburn Rovers for a British record fee of £3.3 million. With all that money in the bank, Southampton bought Ken Monkou and replaced Shearer with three forwards: Kerry Dixon, Dave Speedie and me! I think they got good value from Ken but perhaps the rest of us were a waste of money. The fans were OK to us though. They didn't shout 'Bring back Shearer' or anything. Anyway, I got injured fairly shortly after joining them and that was that as far as I was concerned. I played so few games for them that there was a story in the newspapers that they'd even printed T-shirts down there saying, 'I've Seen Perry Groves Play'.

When I went to Southampton, people said how very focused Shearer had been and how he knew what his career path was going to be. Normally, when a player goes for a big-money move, there is a bit of jealousy, but everyone said what a top bloke he was. No one had a bad word to say about him. He came down to watch a Southampton game when I was injured. There used to be a bar at Southampton that you reached by going up a fire escape to what looked like a tree house. I was in there minding my own business, and he came over and said,

'How are you doing, Perry? You're having a nightmare with your Achilles, aren't you?'

'Yeah,' I said, 'but at least it means I can have a drink!'

He said he hoped everything would turn out OK. As didn't know me, he didn't have to come over, so it was good of him. He didn't buy me a drink, though.

Jack Walker, the Blackburn owner, was buying up all the best English players around at that time – building a team with his cheque-book. Shearer was an obvious player to go for, and, while the sums involved at Blackburn look like peanuts compared to today's transfer fees, it was big money back then.

In his first season at Rovers, Shearer suffered a bad cruciate-ligament injury but still managed to score 16 goals in 21 starts. Rovers' manager Kenny Dalglish was bringing in names like David Batty and Tim Flowers as Blackburn tried to win the title, and the following season they almost made it, only to end as runners-up to Manchester United. Shearer got a very impressive 31 goals and was the football writers' Player of the Year.

It got even better in 1994/95. Chris Sutton was signed and the 'SAS' (Sutton and Shearer) partnership helped Blackburn to the title for the first time since before the First World War. That strike partnership was the main reason Blackburn won the Premiership instead of Manchester United and there was no doubting who was the senior partner in it. He collected the PFA Player of the Year award too.

Remarkably for such a great player, that Premiership winner's gong was the only major honour he won in his long career. There have been a lot worse strikers than him who ended up with a mantelpiece full of trophies. Blackburn couldn't retain it the next season and finished a disappointing seventh, although Shearer was again the Premiership top scorer.

By this time, he was obviously a Most Wanted Man. His name had often been linked with Manchester United, and fellow Geordie Bobby Robson, who was in charge at Barcelona, wanted to take him to Spain. But, all along, there was only going to be one club he would join and in July 1996 he signed for Kevin Keegan and Newcastle United for a world record fee of £15 million. Personally, I think he made a mistake. I think he should have gone to Manchester United and won trophies and then he could have gone to Newcastle. But it shows his single-mindedness.

'The bottom line,' he said, 'is that I've always wanted the challenge of running out in front of the Gallowgate End. I've always said it would be a dream come true if the fans would have me. I might even win back a few of my old mates as well.'

Despite heavy rain, thousands turned up to greet him at St James' Park and he told them, 'I've always said I wanted to play for Newcastle and I can't wait for the first game to come. I think this team is good enough not only to win the Premier League, but to conquer Europe as well. The price tag is nothing at all to do with me. I don't set the price. All I can do is go out and try to do my best and, if that means I score goals, which makes me worth £15 million, that's fine If pressure is going out and enjoying yourself and being sung to by 30,000 or 40,000 fans, then give me more.'

For Shearer, it was one of the saddest – yet paradoxically one of the best – decisions of his life. 'Leaving Blackburn was one of the hardest things I've ever had to do,' he said. 'Jack Walker couldn't have tried any harder to keep me and telling him that I was going was very difficult. I had four years of unbelievable success under some great managers and under Jack Walker, who was a great influence.

'I had a long meeting with him on Sunday and asked if I could see my options, see what I wanted to do. I met Alex Ferguson on Monday and was very impressed with him and then met with the boss on Tuesday and again I was very impressed and, as everyone knows, I always wanted to play for this club at some stage. I want to play for Newcastle with my best years in front of me, whereas, if I'd gone somewhere else for four years, it would then be with my best years behind me.'

The number nine shirt is special to Geordies, with their memories of all-time Newcastle legends Wyn Davies, Malcolm Macdonald and especially their home-grown hero of the 1950s, Jackie Milburn. Shearer understood that well. 'I would play in any number shirt for Newcastle United, but the number nine at Newcastle is something very special and I've always wanted to wear it. I mentioned it to the manager, he mentioned it to Les Ferdinand [their number nine at the time] and Les has been very kind and given it to me.' How diplomatic.

The Newcastle chairman Sir John Hall explained why

they had broken the world record transfer fee. 'We've had a long interest in Shearer. We made a £3 million bid to sign him when he was at Southampton. I don't think their manager at the time would let us speak to him, but then he signed for Blackburn. At that stage, we were still building the club. It's taken a long time to get Alan on board, but everyone is delighted he's coming home.'

The move, Sir John insisted, wasn't about money – it was about bringing a player back to his home-town club. 'But it shows the board's determination to keep Newcastle at the top and to challenge for all the major honours. We've got a great team, but you can always improve on it – and that's what we've done. With Alan and Les Ferdinand linking up, we'll have a lethal duo up front this season.'

That transfer came after a sensational summer for Alan Shearer at the home-based Euro 96. Although he was considered an England regular, injury meant he couldn't play in all the qualifying games for the World Cup of 1994 and that played a part in England's failure to get to the USA tournament. Going into the European Championships two years later, there was even criticism of him because he hadn't scored an international goal since September 1994. A lot of people were saying that he should not be in the side. Shearer himself knew that coach Terry Venables was under pressure to drop him after 12 games without a goal.

It's a measure of Shearer's self-belief that he was to say later, 'I wasn't really surprised when the goals began to flow. I said all along that I never lost confidence in my own ability and often joked that I was saving the goals up for the Championship. The hardest part for me was actually getting myself in the right shape for the finals after an operation on a groin injury at the end of last season.'

That lack of goals was soon remedied in the first half of the opening game against Switzerland. Paul Ince slipped the ball to him inside the area and Shearer gave new meaning to burying the ball in the net. The Swiss goalkeeper was lucky not to get in the way. The game ended in a disappointing 1–1 draw, however, and then the Jocks were the next opponents.

The game is probably best remembered for Paul Gascoigne flicking the ball over Colin Hendry's head and then volleying it to score England's second goal and for Dave Seaman's save from Gary McAllister when the score was 1–0. What a lot of people forget is that the game could have gone either way until Shearer opened the scoring. Gary Neville crossed from the right and you couldn't move for players in the area. That didn't bother Shearer, who just thundered through them all and headed in at the far post. It was a real centre-forward's goal: he kept his eye on the ball all the way, didn't care if there was anything in his path and met it perfectly with his forehead.

There was better to come against the Dutch in the next match. England performances that live on in the memory are few and far between, but this was one of those great nights. It's one thing to beat the Jocks, that's what they're there for, but in recent years the Dutch have turned it on against England. Everyone thought it would be close, but it turned into a massacre.

After 23 minutes, Paul Ince was brought down and

Shearer thumped the penalty hard and low to Edwin van der Sar's right. Teddy Sheringham headed home a corner after 51 minutes, and six minutes later came the best of all. Gazza ran into the penalty area and slipped a pass with the outside of his right foot to Sheringham. He shaped as if to shoot but then rolled it gently sideways for the unmarked Shearer, who had both arms in the air appealing for a pass. Teddy teed it up perfectly, but, where some players would have blasted high and wide, Shearer drilled it into the roof of the net with ferocious power.

England rounded off the night with another goal from Sheringham – in the 20 games he and Alan Shearer played together for England, they notched up 17 goals. If the result was hard to believe, the way England had played was staggering. Just to make it a great evening's work, Patrick Kluivert brought the score-line back to 4–1 near the end, which meant that Scotland failed to qualify for the next round on goals scored. Perfect.

Spain were beaten on penalties in the quarter-final and then we had to play the Germans, didn't we? Shearer was on a roll by this time and, when Tony Adams headed on Gazza's corner after just three minutes, there was your man heading it home. As always, the Germans fought back and we eventually went out on penalties. It's a pity they didn't let Shearer take all our pens. He was always the one Englishman who seemed certain to score no matter how great the pressure was. His penalties were like the rest of his shooting: he just smashed them. He was ice-cool and he didn't try to be clever – there'd be a long run up and then he'd smash it.

He ended up with the Golden Boot award for being the tournament's top scorer and he was undoubtedly the best centre-forward in Europe at this time, if not the world. These days, you don't seem to get the 'focal point' centre-forward which he definitely was – they are not orthodox number nines like he was.

By the 1998 World Cup finals, Shearer was England captain and, although he was sidelined for much of the season before the tournament, he was back by the time they kicked off in France. He scored against Tunisia and then hammered home a penalty in the quarter-final against Argentina. But once David Beckham was sent off the odds were against us and out England went on penalties – again. Unbelievably, that was to be Shearer's only World Cup.

He scored a hat-trick – his only one for England – against Luxembourg in a Euro 2000 qualifier and then the only goal of the game against Germany in the finals, giving England their first competitive win over them since 1966. It wasn't a spectacular goal by any means, but I think it was a great one. David Beckham swung a free-kick in from the right and the German defence allowed it to bounce before Shearer reached it at the far post. There he did what he did all his career: made certain it ended up in the net, this time via his head. But it was a great 'pressure' goal in a big match and that's what he was so good at.

Soon after that, however, came the end of the road as far as England and Alan Shearer were concerned. Before the finals, he announced, 'After a huge amount of thought

I have decided to retire from international football. I would like to play, if selected, in Euro 2000 and then bow out so that the manager has time to plan effectively for the 2002 World Cup. I want everyone to understand that I am not walking away from a challenge – I am hugely patriotic and my time as England captain has made me incredibly proud.

'However, I realise that, if I want to give Newcastle value for money in the remaining four years of my contract with them, I will need to pace myself a bit more than I am able to do at the moment. I am not saying that I would never play for England again – if there was an injury crisis or real need for me to help out, I would always be honoured to answer the call. However, football is about planning for the future and hopefully my decision today will help England become even more successful in the coming years.'

In his 63 appearances, 34 of them as captain, Shearer scored 30 goals, the same as Nat Lofthouse and Tom Finney. Only Bobby Charlton, Gary Lineker, Jimmy Greaves and Michael Owen had scored more.

But if he'd hoped that by not playing for England the honours would start to come to St James' Park, he was wrong. Newcastle are probably the biggest underachievers in British football. They have a fanatical fan-base, large crowds and the facilities to compete with the best. The end result? They haven't won anything of any consequence in the past half-century.

You can't blame Shearer for that. He broke Jackie Milburn's scoring record in the February of his final season, 2005/06, and ended up with 206 goals for the club. His record in the Premiership is, literally, second to none. He scored 260 goals in the top division, a country mile ahead of the man in second place, Andy Cole – sorry 'Andrew' Cole – with 187. Shearer was the top scorer in the Premiership in three seasons and the first player to reach 100 Premiership goals. In the middle of all those goals he had several injuries and cruciate problems with his knee. He lost a yard of pace and that meant he had to remodel his game and use more of his body strength rather than running the channels, and I'm a great admirer of the way he did that.

When he retired himself from the England team he might have started a trend. Normally I'd say that was bollocks – I think you should keep playing for your country no matter what. But he knew his body couldn't take it. He couldn't cope with the extra travelling – he needed the rest and it gave him another three or four years at the top. It's another example of the single-mindedness he showed all along.

No mention of Alan Shearer is complete without commenting on how he looked after himself for all those years when, in the old phrase, 'the boots started flying'. I've already said I didn't think he was a dirty player, although he could look after himself, and I stand by that. One or two other people might disagree.

For a start there's a great clip on the internet under the heading of 'Neil Lennon heinously headbutts Alan Shearer's foot'. The incident took place during a goalless draw with Leicester City when the two tangled on the touchline. Lennon was on the ground and Shearer swung that left boot of his straight into his face, although the ball was nowhere near.

Leicester boss Martin O'Neill declared, 'I don't care if it's Alan Shearer or the Pope – you don't do that kind of thing. My player got kicked in the face deliberately, and Shearer should have been shown the red card. Kenny Dalglish [who was manager at Newcastle by then] has tried to claim there was no malice on Shearer's part, but I don't share that opinion at all. Rules are rules, and video evidence will prove what Shearer did. I was so angry because the referee was only eight yards away, while his linesman had a perfect view of the incident. I don't like seeing anybody sent off. I'm in favour of bodily contact, because this is a man's game. But Shearer was totally out of order, while Neil simply picked himself up and got on with it.'

Not surprisingly Shearer's version was a bit different: 'I have now seen the television pictures of the incident and I am amazed how bad it looks by comparison to what actually happened. I was brought down by Neil Lennon over by the touchline and we both fell clumsily. As I tried to get to my feet I had to really tug my left foot free and the momentum of doing this looked on television like a kick. It certainly wasn't and the fact that Neil is virtually unmarked confirms this. If I did accidentally catch him, I certainly did not mean to. I would never try and deliberately hurt a fellow professional.'

Fair enough, but that was nothing compared to Alan Shearer vs Roy Keane. To put it bluntly, I'd pay to watch it. It's up there with Nigel Benn and Chris Eubank. The two of them tangled numerous times in their careers but the best – sorry, the worst – occasion came at St James' Park when Keano got the ninth red card of his career for taking a swing at Shearer after a little disagreement over a throw-in as Newcastle ran the clock down for a 4–3 victory. After Keane was carded – the second year running he'd been sent off there – he made a bee-line for Shearer, who stood his ground and waited for him to arrive. It took a posse of players to stop it.

'I was sent off for pushing him,' Keane said later, 'but, if you're going to get sent off, you might as well punch him properly because it's the same punishment. Afterwards, I was thinking, You might as well get hung for a sheep as a lamb. It was just a push, though. Ridiculous.'

Shearer's verdict on Keane? 'Sometimes he loses his temper but if you took that away he wouldn't be the player he is and I admire him for that. I've got the utmost respect for Roy Keane. He epitomises everything about the game. He doesn't like losing – and rightly so – but that's what makes him such a great player. I didn't want to get involved. I was just trying to be professional and waste a bit of time, but that's football. But I've got no complaints with him.'

You can't help but feel if he hadn't made it in professional football Alan Shearer would have done all right in the Diplomatic Corps.

CHAPTER 16

MARIO KEMPES

As you've probably noticed, I was football-mad as a kid. I loved to play it and I lived for *Match of the Day* on a Saturday night and a local match on Sunday-afternoon television. And then, to make things even better, every four years along would come this orgy of football called the World Cup to liven up a long Suffolk summer.

I was born in 1965 so I remember bits of the 1970 and 1974 tournaments, but it was the one in Argentina in 1978 that had me glued to the screen. Every game the home nation were in, the pitch was covered in tickertape from their fanatical fans – it looked like giant dandruff everywhere. And one of their players stood head and shoulders (see what I've done there?) above the rest. He was their number ten, Mario Kempes.

He's probably been forgotten by many people who saw those World Cup games. If any Argentineans stick in the memory, they're more likely to be Ossie Ardiles and Ricky Villa, who both came to England and played for Spurs soon afterwards. Younger readers may never have heard of him at all, but as far as I was concerned he was the star of the tournament.

To begin with, you couldn't miss him. Tall and handsome with long legs and flowing hair as black as your hat, he cut a majestic figure. He looked like a matador, which was what they called him. I'd better stop there in case you think this is turning into some boyhood homo-erotic fantasy. It ain't, I can assure you. We didn't go in for that sort of thing in Great Cornard. But no collection of my soccer heroes would be complete without Mario Kempes. He was a giant of a man and when he had the ball at his feet he seemed to be challenging anyone to have the courage to tackle him.

Even back then, there was something about the Argies. They were dark, unshaven, hard men with unbelievable skills and a volatile side to them lurking just below everything they did. I think they are to the Brazilians as the Scots are to the English; they have a chip on their shoulders over the relationship and no matter how hard they try they can't get over it.

Nowadays, you can't go to a Premiership ground or watch a Champions League game without seeing an Argentinean, so that air of unease about them isn't as strong as it used to be, but back in the 1970s these unknown figures mainly stayed at home. Kempes was the only one earning a living abroad – he'd joined Spanish side Valencia a year before the tournament after scoring 86 goals in 107 games for Rosario Central.

In 1978, the Argentineans had never won the World Cup and, as they were the host nation, this was to be their best chance. Their manager was a long-haired, chain-smoking figure called Cesar Luis Menotti, who was so confident of the strength of his squad he decided to leave out the 17-year-old wonderkid of Argentinean football. The boy's name? Diego Maradona. But you could see where Menotti was coming from. As well as Villa and Ardiles, he had a tough captain in defender Daniel Passarella and a courageous striker called Leopoldo Luque, who sported the kind of drooping moustache you don't see any more and who should have been working as a villain in a spaghetti western.

And then there was Kempes, of whom Menotti said, 'He's strong, he's got skill, he creates spaces and he shoots hard. He's a player who can make a difference, and he can play in a centre-forward position.'

It wasn't the kind of centre-forward we were used to seeing in England, though. He seemed to roam all over the opponents' half, going wherever he pleased instead of ploughing the penalty-box furrow like a John Toshack.

But, as often happens, the host nation started badly and ended up second in their group behind Italy. That meant they had to play the next round away from Buenos Aires. Kempes, their main hope for goals, hadn't scored in the first three games.

Menotti, who liked to think of himself as a bit of an intellectual, thought he had the answer, as Kempes recalled later. 'We were so focused on the task in hand [that] we never left the training camp, and I couldn't be bothered with shaving. After nearly three weeks I had a pretty decent beard and moustache. I played like that in our first two games, but shaved the beard off before our third. We were heading back to our camp after that match when the coach said, "Mario, why don't you get rid of the moustache and see if your luck changes?"

'The coach had been over to see me before the World Cup to see how I was getting on in Valencia. At that time I was clean-shaven. "You didn't have a beard or moustache when you were playing for Valencia," he said to me, "so why don't you shave when we get to Rosario and you might start scoring again?" I took his advice and ended up scoring twice that day [against Poland]. That marked the start of a new chapter for me. After that every time he saw me, he'd say, "You're due a shave today, Mario, aren't you?"'

And with the next three matches being played in Rosario – the city where he'd begun his career – 'El Matador' came to life. After he'd scored both goals in the 2–0 victory over Poland, there was a 0–0 draw with Brazil and then the third and crucial qualifying game. The Argentineans needed to beat a good Peruvian side by a hatful to get into the final and they did it with ease. Rather too much ease, said the suspicious Brazilians. They had a point: Peru had a good side yet they rolled over as the Argies scored at will past Peru's Argentinean-born goalkeeper. Stewards' or what? But what did I know or care about that? All I knew was that Kempes had scored another two goals in the 6–0 bum-smacking.

That brought the Argies up against Holland in the final. The Dutch, who were in the final for the second tournament running, didn't have Johan Cruyff, but they still had most of their other players from four years earlier and they were determined not to be bullied out of the game. The match even started with a row over a lightweight cast on winger Rene van de Kerkhof's arm and that delayed the kick-off.

Despite a strong Dutch start, Kempes was the hero for the vast majority of the 71,000 crowd as he tapped home the opening goal after strong running by Luque and Ardiles. Substitute Dick Nanninga headed an equaliser ten minutes from time but you could tell it wasn't going to be Holland's day when Rob Rensenbrink's shot hit the post in the last minute. In extra-time, Kempes took a grip on the game and every time he got the ball you could see the fear in the Dutch. Eventually, he beat and barged his way past three men to bundle the ball past the keeper Jan Jongbloed to put Argentina ahead in the 105th minute. He then set up winger Daniel Bertoni five minutes from time to make it 3–1 to Argentina. That was the end of the scoring, and joy, as they say, was unconfined. Cue more dandruff.

Kempes later said that the highlight of that World Cup was the players' rapport with the crowd all the way through. 'Even when we lost against Italy in the first round, they kept on singing. It was incredible. Every time I went on to the pitch, I had goose bumps. From the pitch, you can't see individual faces but you can hear all the shouts getting louder and louder as the game goes on. The final was incredible. We were all on a cloud. I've never felt such emotion as I did then. The people's fervour was exceptional: it was really something beautiful.'

El Matador also ended up as the tournament's top scorer with six goals and was also voted 1978's South American Footballer of the Year. Oh, and as well as winning the trophy, the Argentineans also won the FIFA Fair Play award. That's like Switzerland winning a 'Services to the War' award.

After becoming a world champion, Kempes returned to Valencia, where he had two successful spells – one either side of a year with River Plate in 1981, when they won the Argentinean championship – making 247 appearances and scoring 146 goals. He was back in Spain in time for the World Cup in 1982, but his third and final World Cup tournament ended in disappointment. Kempes didn't score – despite having his barnet cut – and the Argies went home early after the second group stage. That was the end of his international career, during which he scored 20 goals in 43 appearances.

He later moved to a smaller Spanish club, Hercules, before winding down his career in Austrian, Chilean and even Indonesian football as a player-manager. He finally retired in 1996 at the age of 41, but was fresh enough in Pele's mind eight years later to be included in the great man's list of 125 greatest living footballers.

For his final World Cup in Spain, the Argentineans numbered their players alphabetically by surname, so bizarrely Ardiles had the number one on his back. They made an exception for just one player who said he wanted to wear his favourite number ten. No, it wasn't Kempes – it was Maradona who insisted on having it. No prizes for guessing who I think looked better in it – El Matador.

CHAPTER 17

MATT LE TISSIER

Half the goals I scored for Southampton were created by Matt Le Tissier. I remember all the details vividly, as if it were yesterday. Mind you, it would be pretty hard to forget as I only scored two and I broke a toe scoring one of them. The goal that I managed to emerge from in one piece, however, still sticks in my mind. If things had gone right, it should have been the first of many, or at least the first of quite a few.

I hadn't requested a move from Arsenal to Southampton but when George Graham said they had come in for me I decided quickly – too quickly really – to move to The Dell. My money was going to be better and as I was increasingly on the fringe at Arsenal it seemed, as they say, a good idea at the time.

One of the things I was genuinely excited about, though, was playing with Matt Le Tissier. He was, quite simply, a class act. One of the elements of his game I really admired was the way, with hardly any back-lift, he could hit long balls into the stride of forwards as they were moving at pace – just right for me. When I'd met the Southampton manager Ian Branfoot he'd talked about how his vision was to play Le Tiss wide out left and me wide out right and then Matt would find me with those diagonal passes of his that he'd hit as if he had an anvil in his boots.

The goal he made for me would nowadays be described as 'scored by Groves, assist by Le Tissier' and it came against Leeds United. They had been champions of the old First Division the season before, 1991/92, so they were hard to beat. Their left-back was Tony Dorigo, a good player who won 15 England caps and in the normal course of events he'd have won more, but at first Kenny Sansom blocked his way into the England team and then along came Stuart Pearce, so he became stuntman for him.

Dorigo probably took a cushion with him to sit on when he joined the England squad as he'd spend more time sitting on the bench than playing, but I admire that attitude. He wouldn't think of retiring from international football just because he couldn't get a regular place in the starting line-up, like precious people such as Jamie Carragher at Liverpool. You know the sort: they think it's beneath them to be selected for an elite squad of the best 23 players in the country. They're on too much money to be bothered playing for England.

Anyway, when they came to The Dell as reigning champions we knew we had a game on our hands. Le

Tiss picked the ball up on the left wing, had a quick look and then pinged a ball through to me that must have travelled almost 50 yards before it curled inside Dorigo. I took one touch and then stuck it left-footed past John Lukic, my old mate from Arsenal days, and inside his left-hand post.

For me, it was then downhill all the way from there on. I knew that if I made a run Le Tiss would find me, but I never played with him enough to build up an understanding. I got injured and spent most of my time at Southampton either on crutches or trying to get fit again. It didn't happen though and I had to retire.

Of course I was aware of Matt Le Tissier before I was transferred, but he had never torn us apart at Arsenal. We played a high tempo game and Lee Dixon and Nigel Winterburn always kept tight on him so we handled him well. But it was obvious that he was Southampton's most dangerous player and when I was transferred I could see at close quarters just how good he was. We trained a lot together and he would do two or three things in every session that took your breath away. Considering that he was half-a-stone overweight and looked like he was in slow motion, he still somehow managed to glide past players and change his pace or change feet without even trying. He made it all look so easy. He was a bit of a lazy bastard in training but he knew that he could get away with it.

The truth is that he was probably born an era too late. He should have been playing at the same time as Rodney Marsh or Stan Bowles, players like that. Yet his top 25 to

30 goals would be up there with the best that Thierry Henry could manage, they were that good.

Southampton had had some famous players in their past – but not too many. The club record number of appearances, 713, belonged to winger Terry Paine, who had been part of the England World Cup squad of 1966, and striker Mick Channon held the goalscoring record. They had also had Kevin Keegan and Peter Shilton for a spell, but if you ask any Southampton fan today who their greatest player was they will tell you it was Le Tiss. When I went there, it was as though he was the mayor of Southampton. It wasn't long before the fans started calling him 'Le God'!

He was born on the Channel Island of Guernsey and, after he'd had a trial at Oxford United, he signed for Southampton and stayed there throughout his career. In total he turned out 540 times for them and scored 209 goals, including 48 out of the 49 penalties he took and that is a phenomenal success rate. In the 1993/94 season, he hit 30 goals, which was pretty good as Southampton were struggling, and that wasn't all that unusual either. He won the *Match of the Day* Goal of the Season award a year later when he scored from 40 yards against Blackburn Rovers with what you could almost call a 'powerful lob' over his old Southampton mate Tim Flowers. The keeper ended half in the net, half wrapped round the goalpost – not a pretty sight.

It was one of a pair that he scored that day and it obviously gave him a great deal of satisfaction to score past his old chum. He even grinned and pointed out to him that he shouldn't have come off his line. Southampton still lost 3–2, although the Blackburn manager Kenny Dalglish did say, 'Le Tissier's second goal was obviously a wonderful goal. I think it would have been more of an individual effort from him if it had resulted in three points – but it could win Goal of the Season.'

Le Tiss also memorably lobbed Peter Schmeichel of Manchester United, something it looked physically impossible to do. In fact, he seemed to specialise in spectacular goals – tap-ins weren't his style. He probably couldn't be arsed to run with the ball any more so he'd go for goal.

I was long gone by the time Le Tiss scored the final goal at The Dell in a 3–2 victory over Arsenal in May 2001, before Southampton moved grounds. He had been injured for much of the season and came on as substitute, notching the winner with a left-foot volley from outside the area. He played some games at the new ground, St Mary's Stadium, before injuries got the better of him and he called it a day in 2002.

That was still ten years away when I moved to Southampton, though. I soon discovered that there were three groups among the players at the club. There would be the younger players like Jason Dodd, Jeff Kenna, Richard Hall, Nicky Banger and Neil Maddison, and then there was the group of more experienced pros like Micky Adams, Glen Cockerill, Kevin Moore, Tim Flowers and Iain Dowie. Matt would float between those two groups.

The third group, which included me, was made up of the recent signings who'd been bought with the transfer money from Alan Shearer's move to Blackburn Rovers. That included Dave Speedie, Kerry Dixon and Ken Monkou. Terry Hurlock was a fairly new arrival too. It hadn't been like that at Arsenal – there had been no cliques there – so it was something that I had to get used to.

There was also resentment because the players already there knew that people coming in from big clubs would be on better money than them. That always happens and, although Le Tiss wasn't one of them, there was a feeling of unease about it. I guess I didn't help the situation by being loud and brash – they thought I was a Cockney wide-boy coming in. At first they were under the impression I was playing the big star – it took them three or four months to realise it was just my character and by that time I was injured.

Le Tiss was very confident and sure of his ability. He knew that he was the main man but in no way was he a big-time Charlie. He was also a very intelligent guy and his laidback demeanour hid that intelligence. He wasn't like a Graham Le Saux who'd carry the *Guardian* with him all the time but he was sharp and witty and didn't have to prove anything by reading Tolstoy on the coach.

Instead, he was in the club's card school, just playing for fivers or tenners, which would hardly buy you a cup of coffee by today's standards. They usually played Hearts but I wasn't normally included. I didn't want to be, as I think cards are boring, but sometimes if they were a player short, because someone was out of the squad or was injured, I would be asked to join in as I knew the rules.

When I messed up, they would all turn on me like a pack of wolves, so, being the mature, grown-up person I am, I'd end up telling them to stick their game up their arse.

My one criticism of Le Tiss was that he was a big fish in a small pond. I thought that if I had had his natural ability I would not have been content playing my entire career at a provincial club like Southampton. I would have wanted to test myself at a higher level. By staying at Southampton, he could have four or five bad games on the trot and still get selected. He could have a dump in the centre spot and the fans would sing his name.

In his autobiography, he says he rejected moves to AC Milan and Chelsea, and he was often linked with Spurs. If he'd gone to any of the three, he'd probably have had a chance of winning some cups at least. But he would always have been under scrutiny from the fans and the media, and he probably didn't fancy it. Ability would not have been the problem but I think mentally it would have been – that is where the difficulties would have arisen. People don't realise the different level you have to be on at a big club. You have to be able to handle it. At the time I couldn't understand it, but as I've got older I realise that he was simply happy where he was.

Sadly, his England career never really got started. He was only capped eight times in four years and never scored. He did manage a hat-trick for England B against Russia (he also hit the bar twice) shortly before the 1998 World Cup, but Glenn Hoddle didn't even name him in the squad for the finals. As he was born in the Channel Islands, Matt could have played for any of the Home

Nations – perhaps he should have tried his luck with another one of them.

When he did retire, the manager of Southampton, Gordon Strachan, said, 'Matt has been the best Southampton footballer ever. Luckily we live in the video age where we'll be able to see that brilliance for ever. Think of Southampton and it's Matt Le Tissier, yachting and the *Titanic*. They've built better boats since, but there'll only ever be one Matt Le Tissier. This club will never see a player as talented as him again, I'm convinced of it, so we should enjoy that.'

Le Tiss was realistic about it all. 'In the end, it was not a hard decision. It has been terribly frustrating at times [and] an increasing trend over the last three years, with one niggling injury after another. Even if the club offered me a contract for sentimental reasons, I could not take money under false pretences. If I thought I could play on at my best, then that would be different, but my body is not so much giving me hints as screaming at me. … I would hate another season like this one where I spend my whole time desperately trying to get fit and then breaking down as soon as I play. Besides, it's playing havoc with my golf!

'It is a sad day but I feel better now I have finally made the decision. I have had 17 great years with the club and have some very special memories but now I am looking forward to a new chapter in my life.'

Shortly after he retired, he joined former Prime Minister David Lloyd George, Lord Kitchener and Saints club president Ted Bates in being given the Freedom of

Southampton. He deserved it and I'm not jealous. I don't think my 15 appearances for the Saints put me in the running for a gong anyway.

And, in case you're wondering, my other goal for Southampton was a volley against Wimbledon. And yes, it did hurt when I broke my toe. Cheers, Vinny!

CHAPTER 18

CRISTIANO RONALDO

Cristiano Ronaldo arrived in England with a reputation of being a poser. There was no end product – it was just step-over, step-over, dive. Of course, he was a flair player but no one in a million years thought he'd end up scoring 42 goals in one season – from the left wing. I thought he might be in the same vein as Anders Limpar had been at Arsenal in the early 1990s, but without the impact that he'd had. Got that one right, didn't I?

What I didn't realise is just how tough mentally Ronaldo proved to be, and that's what has turned him into a great player. Look at the way he handled the 'winking' affair from the World Cup in 2006. Wayne Rooney, his Manchester United room-mate no less, had just been tackled by Ricardo Carvalho and had stamped on him – sort of – as a result. Ronaldo got involved, there was a bit of shoving, Ronaldo and the rest of the

Portuguese decided to tell the ref what action to take and Rooney got a red card as a result. As he left the field, the cameras caught Ronaldo's wink of satisfaction. Ten-men England held on for another 30 minutes of extra-time but then naturally lost the penalty shoot-out – and just to rub it in it was Ronaldo's spot-kick that finished it off.

I don't blame Wayne Rooney for what he did. It wasn't a sending-off offence anyway – he should just have got a yellow card. As for Ronaldo, he was young and immature and he shouldn't have got involved. If it had been me and my old Arsenal pal Paul Merson on opposite sides, I'd have badgered the referee to 'Get him off, he's a thug' but I would have been joking when I said it.

It wasn't a joke when Ronaldo said it, though, and all hell broke loose afterwards. 'Yes, I speak to referee,' he said, 'but I say, "Foul!" I don't say, "Red card." I don't care who says that. It is not true.'

Rooney's version of events was, not too surprisingly, a bit different. 'I want to say absolutely categorically that I did not intentionally put my foot down on Ricardo Carvalho. He slid in from behind me and unfortunately ended up in a position where my foot was inevitably going to end up as I kept my balance. That's all there was to it. If you ask any player and indeed almost any fan, they will tell you that I am straight and honest in the way I play.

'From what I've seen in the World Cup, most players would have gone to ground at the slightest contact but my only thought then was to keep possession for England. When the referee produced the red card I was amazed –

gobsmacked. I bear no ill feeling to Cristiano but am disappointed that he chose to get involved. I suppose I do, though, have to remember that on that particular occasion we were not team-mates.'

The ref said he wasn't influenced by anyone, but if I'd been Rooney I'd have larruped Ronaldo in the first training session back at Old Trafford.

We all love a pantomime villain, don't we? And that's what Ronaldo became the next season. But it didn't seem to bother him one bit and I admire that in a player. It shows great mental strength and courage to ignore all that. What the crowd who are giving out stick don't realise is that all they are doing to the top players is making them more determined than ever to turn it on. And that's exactly what he did when he came back to the Premiership and the Champions League – he simply turned it on. He showed that something special he'd had all his life.

He was born on Madeira, an island nearly 600 miles from the Portuguese mainland, and his childhood home, a bungalow, was so small that the washing machine was on the roof. His family weren't exactly poverty-stricken but he did have it tough from an early age because he was named after US President Ronald Reagan, which can't have been very common out there.

By the time he was 11, he'd been spotted by Sporting Lisbon and he joined their academy. The first time he ever flew was to leave Madeira and fly to Portugal to move into digs with nine other boys. He was in tears at leaving and eventually Sporting paid to fly his mother over to comfort him. 'There were a lot of tears in my first few weeks in Lisbon,' he said. 'Madeira is so small. I couldn't believe the traffic and noise of a capital city. In the beginning, nobody could understand me because of my accent and I couldn't understand them. I used to call my family whenever I could. I remember buying phone cards and looking at the units go down as I spoke to my parents and brothers and sisters.'

But he stuck it out and at 16 he was in the Sporting first team. In the summer of 2003 – shortly after he'd turned 18 – he ran riot down both wings as his side beat Manchester United 3–1 in a pre-season tournament. It didn't come as a complete shock to United, though, as they had already been tracking him since before Christmas, with chief scout Mick Brown and Sir Alex Ferguson's brother Martin, the club's European scout, becoming regulars at Sporting's matches. When United beat Chelsea and Arsenal to his signature that summer, Ronaldo became the most expensive teenager in British football at £12 million.

'After we played Sporting Lisbon last week, the lads in the dressing room talked about him constantly,' Fergie said. 'And on the plane back from the game, they urged me to sign him. That's how highly they rated him.' The United boss was sure he'd found a star. 'He's one of the most exciting young players I've seen. He is extremely talented, a two-footed attacker who can play anywhere up front, right, left or through the middle.'

When he signed for them Ronaldo didn't want to wear the number seven shirt that had been worn by such players as Bryan Robson, Eric Cantona and David Beckham. He felt it would be too much of a responsibility, he has said, 'but Alex Ferguson said, "No, you're going to have number seven" and the famous shirt was an extra source of motivation. I was forced to live up to such an honour.'

A lot of the publicity Ronaldo has received has centred on his 'diving'. Middlesbrough manager Gareth Southgate said after a penalty was awarded against his team, 'We feel cheated. It's as simple as that. My view is the complete opposite to Sir Alex Ferguson. The lad has got a history of doing it. It was never a penalty. There was clearly no contact and our keeper tried to get out of his way. I don't blame the referee because it happened at speed, but it has cost us dearly. It's hard when you go behind to a goal like that. It happened with a free-kick when he went down again. How many times are we going to see this sort of thing? The answer is for players to perform in the manner they should. If they have the opportunity to stay on their feet and not go down for a penalty, they should.'

Ferguson said, 'I thought it was a clear penalty.' Shock!

A month or so later, Spurs had a similar complaint when Ronaldo went down near Steed Malbranque. Their manager, Martin Jol, insisted the 45th-minute penalty should not have been given and the Tottenham fans turned on Ronaldo after the break, having seen replays of the flashpoint from three different angles on the big screen at half-time.

'It wasn't a penalty,' Jol said. 'Malbranque stuck his

foot out then pulled it back. I can't say he took advantage of it but I don't know. … It's about the referee – he has to make a decision. He is a human being. He had a good view of it. At first, I thought he was falling over but, if you see it again, Malbranque has stuck his foot out. That is probably what the referee saw but he didn't see that Malbranque pulled his foot back as well. I wouldn't say that Ronaldo was diving but it was a difficult situation. If you see it on television, you see that it's no penalty.'

While everyone was having a go at Ronaldo over such incidents – and there were many more of them – he went up in my estimation for a simple reason. He was Public Enemy Number One but he didn't let it affect his game – he got even better! What a lot of people assume is that, because he is a 'flair' player, he must be slightly built. But he is 6ft 1in tall and to have him coming at you full-tilt doing his step-overs must be like trying to stop a charging rhino. I don't think he 'dives' as much as he did when he first arrived here, but he still keeps winning penalties and opposing managers still complain about the unfairness of it all.

Ronaldo's level of play since that World Cup has been staggering and a lot of the credit for that has to go down to Alex Ferguson. His man-management has always been superb, and just look at the way he has taken care of Ronaldo. At first there was all that criticism of his 'showboating' and then the hatred from Rooney's sending off. On top of that he is always being linked with Real Madrid, but every time Ferguson seems to put a protective arm around him and say, 'Come on home to the family that is Manchester United, son.'

This is what Ferguson said after one bout of speculation that he would be off to Real as the most expensive footballer in the world: 'After the meeting I had with Cristiano, when I explained the situation and what we expect of players from Manchester United, he's already said he's delighted to be back here, so to say that he's here reluctantly is not the case. When we had the meeting the lad quickly agreed with me, so I have no issues whatsoever with him. [One on one in a room with Fergie – he ain't going to argue, is he?] He'll be OK, he'll do his best, he'll be a great player this season because he's still improving. He'll be absolutely fantastic for us.

'Everyone said last season that he wouldn't score more than the 23 goals he scored in the previous campaign. I don't think anyone thought he could do better than that and I said he would. I expected him to improve and I expect him to improve again this season. Of course, we're at a different level – 42 goals against 23 goals is completely different – so if he gets to 41 goals I think we'll forgive him.'

It's a technique that works.

Everyone rates Ronaldo as a player. Eusebio, the most famous Portugal international of them all, reckons Ronaldo may overtake him. 'The way he's going at the moment he can become not only the best footballer in Portugal, but also the best in the world. Maybe not the best of all time, but I think within a short space of time Ronaldo will be recognised as the best footballer in the world.'

Johan Cruyff said, 'For me, Ronaldo is above the rest

and if he keeps scoring in this rhythm and stays in this sort of form then he will prove that he is the best. Ronaldo is better than George Best and Denis Law, who were two brilliant and great players in the history of United. But Ronaldo is 22 and, with his quality and progression in the game, I believe he will be even better and win many more prizes for himself and his club. For him to be so good takes dedication. But he also needs support from his team-mates and his coach, Sir Alex Ferguson.

'The only thing that I see as a weakness in his game is the number of assists, but he is young enough and has the right coach to improve in that respect. He scores great goals and now also spectacular free-kicks, but to be the complete forward he must provide more assists as his record can be improved.'

I too think Ronaldo is on the verge of greatness. Well, I'm not going to argue with Johan Cruyff, am I? I'd agree with the gist of what he said, but there is a criticism of him that, although he tears most teams apart, he has not turned it on against the very best in the really big games. Even so, this hasn't stopped him picking up a clutch of awards such as Player of the Year, Young Player of the Year, European Player of the Year… You name it, he's won it.

One aspect of his game I haven't mentioned, though, is his heading ability. It's fantastic. He climbs high and he's as brave as they come when he goes for the ball. Some great flair players have lacked that part of their game, but not him. It's surprising in one respect. With all that gel on his barnet, you'd think he wouldn't want to mess his hair up, would you?

CHAPTER 19

PAUL McGARTH

I played against Paul McGrath loads of times. He really was a colossus. There was never any screaming or spitting or snarling or 'I'll break your legs'. He wasn't 'I'll do this, I'll do that' to you, in the Graham Roberts or Paul Miller category. He was certainly tough – he was a hard man, all right – but he didn't go out to prove himself. He had an unbelievable desire to win a game of football, to put himself on the line.

Paul McGrath didn't do step-overs. He didn't do fancy juggling skills and he didn't smash the ball in from 30 yards. Some spectators would hardly notice him during the entire 90 minutes. It was only when the final whistle went that they might realise that he hadn't put a foot wrong throughout the entire match – that he hadn't made a single mistake.

He didn't look particularly quick when he ran. He had

an unusual style – very low to the ground, a loping style – so it didn't look as though he was covering the ground very quickly. But obviously he was, because no one could ever do him for pace. I was quick, but every time you thought you'd got past him down a channel or knocked the ball past him, this Inspector Gadget leg would come out and slide-tackle you. But nine times out of ten he wasn't content to put the ball out of play so he could get applause from the crowd for a great tackle – instead, he'd come away with the ball, bring it out of defence and use it. He's probably best remembered as a centre-back, but he also played midfield for Manchester United and Ireland, and you don't get to do that without a lot of ability. But wherever he played, either at centre-half or in central midfield, he was smoothly efficient and with a steeliness about him.

I don't profess to know him as a friend, but I know from being in his company and from what David O'Leary and Niall Quinn at Arsenal said about him from their time together with the Irish side that he's a very quiet and unassuming man. He's very shy and I think that's what led to a lot of his well-publicised drinking problems. If you ask people like David O'Leary, Paul was not one of those drunks who got aggressive or nasty or violent and would want a fight – it just made him more confident. He was normally very shy and so when he had a few sherbets he would start talking to people and not be so withdrawn.

It's difficult not to put at least some of this lack of self-confidence down to his childhood. A lot of famous footballers think they had a tough start in life, but, compared to Paul McGrath's, they had silver spoons in their mouths from the day they came into the world.

Paul was to become one of the most famous Irish players of all time, yet he was born in that famous Irish beauty spot of Ealing in West London. The reason for that was simple: he had an Irish mother and a Nigerian father, and his mum was terrified about her family's reaction to her having a child by a black man so she travelled to London to have the baby in secret. When he was a few weeks old, he was placed with an adoption agency and spent his childhood going from one Dublin orphanage to another, although he was later to be reunited with his mother.

Paul played for St Patrick's Athletic in Dublin but he didn't turn full-time until he was 22. Until then he earned a living in the real world as a steel worker, making giant metal security gates with spikes on and then having to haul them around, and as a security guard. He never forgot those early days.

In 1982, a year after he'd turned professional, he signed for Ron Atkinson's Manchester United, who'd been keeping tabs on him since his junior days. It took him a couple of years to establish himself in the first team, however. United had Kevin Moran, Gordon McQueen and Martin Buchan at the time, and Paul also had injury problems. In fact, injuries were to plague him throughout his career.

Still, he was a member of the 1985 United side that won the FA Cup, beating Everton 1–0 in extra-time. His big day was marred somewhat by his poor pass that led to centre-back Kevin Moran committing the foul which resulted in his becoming the first player to be sent off in a Cup Final. But Moran, his room-mate, never bore a grudge and McGrath certainly atoned by keeping both Andy Gray and Graeme Sharp under control as Norman Whiteside scored the late winner.

Even then Paul felt very self-conscious, remembering the team celebrations in a rather different way than most cup-winners do. 'The bit that sticks out is when we grouped for the photograph. I had seen this done time and time again but I just couldn't get into it ... I've watched it on the video a few times since and I'm just so conscious of what we were doing. We were jumping up and down, trying to sing this song and I'm thinking, Am I bouncing right? Will this look OK? I had just won an FA Cup medal but I just couldn't get into the spirit of things.'

Two years later, he has said, alcohol was dominating his life. 'By 1987, I was drinking for fun. We weren't supposed to drink two days before a game but, if I went out on the Wednesday, I would wake up feeling that bad that I would have to have a drink just to get through Thursday. And suddenly it would be Friday, the day before the game and I'd think, You've just got to leave it alone, but inevitably I'd push it right to the limit. And then I'd run out and face top-quality people who've been on pasta diets all week.

'There was a couple of times, at Villa in particular, when I'd be sitting in the dressing room before a game with the comedowns and the jitters and I'd be feeling so scared that I'd have to ask the lads for a bit of a dig-out. And they always did. But it was a horrendous way to live as a sportsman, living like that, living on the edge. Some people say there's an excitement to living on the edge but it wasn't very exciting for me. It was horrendous.' Just think – all the times he crash-tackled me he was on the DTs. What a man.

When Alex Ferguson took over at United in 1986, he was determined to break the drinking culture that existed there. All the teams around that time had a drink culture: Arsenal did, Manchester United did, Liverpool did too. But, as everyone was at it, you had a level playing field. Bryan Robson, Norman Whiteside and Paul have been publicly nicknamed The Booze Brothers and their antics have been well reported in the past.

Ron Atkinson said of them, 'When I was at Manchester United, Norman Whiteside, Paul McGrath and Bryan Robson were like angels. Bryan always liked a drink but at the right time. For my money, that drinking happened when I'd left the club and they were out with long-term injuries. I'll tell you what, if they were drinking, I wish the rest of them were out drinking with them. They were our three best players by a mile.'

Paul McGrath once recalled the ongoing struggle he had with Ferguson when he said in an interview, 'We were on a collision course, me and Alex, because he was out to seize control of the club by barking at everyone. He had me and Norman in the office all the time, shouting and fining us, but it didn't work. We were injured a lot of the time and we'd be at a loss after rehabilitation work in the morning, so inevitably we'd end up on a bar-stool in the afternoon saying, "Aw, let's just go for it."

'I'd had lots of knee operations by then and Alex thought, Hang on, this is a drinker with rotten knees... He was right and, if I'd been him, I'd have kicked me and Norman out a long time before then. He saved me in a way. When he let me go to Villa, something welled up in me and I wanted to prove I could really play. The next five years, whenever Villa played United, we walked past each other in the corridor. And then we beat United in the [1994] League Cup Final and, afterwards, Alex put his hand out and said, "Well done, big man." It made me wish I had gone up to him first.'

In his autobiography, Alex Ferguson wrote, 'I found him unreachable. Time and again I would have him into my office, attempting to bring home to him the damage that alcohol was doing to his life. He would sit there and just nod in agreement, then walk out the door and carry on as before, seemingly indifferent to the threat his behaviour posed to a career already jeopardised by chronic knee problems.

'The methods that had served me so well over the years in dealing with the serious personal difficulties of players achieved nothing with him. But I went on trying, for my sake as well as his. I knew that a fit McGrath who had his head straight would be a huge asset to Manchester United. He was an exceptionally skilful and stylish defender, with marvellous innate athleticism, a man whose abilities stood comparison with those of any central defender in the game. But his dishevelled lifestyle had taken its toll. In the match that was my first as United manager, that 2–0 defeat at Oxford, I had been advised to play him in midfield but he did not have the stamina for the job. He was so knackered that I had to take him off. Centre-half was the right position for him and if he had given himself a chance he could have flourished there.'

There was even talk of Paul quitting the game before that transfer to Aston Villa in August 1989. He was drinking a lot, the injuries were already there and he was almost 30. Yet, if anything, the best years of his playing career were about to begin. In that first season at Aston Villa, they almost won the title, losing out narrowly to Liverpool, and a couple of seasons later they were runners-up again. In 1991, he was reunited with Ron Atkinson at Villa, where the supporters had taken to referring to their new hero as God. It's a miracle that 'God' ever got on the pitch at all, given what was happening in his private life. He described his drinking habits like this: 'Social drinking doesn't interest me. I don't want to sit at a bar and drink with people until I am merry. I drink for a blackout. I drink until I can't function.' Now, that's hardcore by any standards.

He'd disappear for days and not know where he'd been and he admitted to playing at the highest level while still suffering the effects of drink. He reckoned he played ten games while suffering from a hangover and a couple while actually drunk. In one of those, he had to mark Alan Shearer. Shearer didn't score, probably anaesthetised by his breath.

'It's difficult to explain the desperation that kicks in when the cravings hit,' Paul has said. 'You end up needing something to give you a blackout. Anything. So I took out a pint glass and filled it with Domestos. What I was thinking, I haven't got a clue, but everything was quite deliberate. I remember screwing the top back on the container, then looking at the glass, knowing I was about to play Russian Roulette with my life. Then I did it. Took the glass and downed the Domestos in one go.'

After waking up in agony, he only survived by drinking large amounts of water. A few years later, he got so desperate he drank Domestos again and was saved that time by being violently sick. He also became addicted to tranquillisers and once slashed his wrists with a Stanley knife. He played wearing wristbands to hide the wounds.

When Ron Atkinson arrived at Villa, Paul was doing practically no training. Atkinson would just say to him, 'What do you want to do this week?'

Paul himself said in one interview that after a few months at Villa he stopped training – and didn't train properly for the next seven years! 'The Villa physio Jim Walker, who is more than a friend, he is a hero of mine, is basically the one that kept my career going. If I hadn't had Jim on my side, I would have probably finished playing about four seasons earlier than I did.

'Jim created a regime where I just went in and did 10 minutes on the bike each morning and that was about it. Some days I would just have a bath. The games would look after my fitness. It was hard not to join in with the rest of the guys' training, especially the five-a-sides, which I used to love. I'd just watch them and collect the balls. But the lads at Villa were brilliant: none of them moaned about it, they just accepted it.'

Atkinson let him do what he wanted because he knew his performances on a Saturday would be outstanding.

When I was at Southampton, I remember he was in the Villa squad when they came to play us at The Dell. I was injured at the time – what a surprise – but I sat in on the team-talk and our manager Ian Branfoot talked quite a bit about Paul as he was obviously one of Villa's best players. Soon afterwards, I was busy handing out the complimentary tickets when I saw the Villa team bus arrive. Paul McGrath was the last one off and he could hardly get down the steps of the coach.

I went straight to see Ian Branfoot and told him, 'You might as well relax. Paul McGrath is a raspberry ripple. He won't be playing.'

Soon after that, the team sheets came through and his name was on it, but I still went on about the state he was in and that we could take advantage of it. You can guess what happened next: he was the best player on the park by a country mile. He was crashing in with tackles, unbeatable in the air, a colossus. Another of my great pre-match predictions! Yet after the game was finished he had a stone in his shoe again.

Paul also became a hero in Ireland for his exploits for the national side. He won his first cap for Ireland against Italy in 1985 (the year of that FA Cup Final win) and his last 12 years later against Wales – 83 caps and eight goals later. He was at the heart of the Irish team's success stories during those years: the country's first appearance in the European Championships in 1988, when only eight teams reached the finals, and two World Cups in 1990 and 1994.

The highlight of the 1988 matches was the 1–0 defeat of England, and in the 1990 World Cup in Italy the Irish were only knocked out 1–0 by the host team after the Republic had drawn with England in the group stage. Early in the Italy game, Paul ran at the brilliant AC Milan defender Franco Baresi and tried a trick he sometimes used of shouting when he got near the man on the ball to upset him. To his surprise, it did: Baresi was taken aback. At the end of the tournament his performances were recognised by his being named in the World XI of best players.

The World Cup in America four years later elevated him to even greater stature among the Irish fans. He was a hero in their 1–0 victory over Italy, the eventual runners-up, in what was probably his country's most famous victory. His performance, especially against striker Roberto Baggio, has entered Irish folklore. While on all fours and seemingly out of the game, he decided to stop a Baggio half-volley by putting his face in front of the ball. After it had struck him full on, he simply got to his feet and chased after it. As the Ireland defender Terry Phelan said, 'You look at Paul McGrath and he's got two bad knees, but he'll give anyone a run for their money. He's as strong as an ox and he just won everything in the air against the Italians.'

His earlier verbal assault on Baresi hadn't led to any grudges: the Italian great has said that by 1994 McGrath was 'the best defender in the world'. His manager with Ireland during those vintage years was Jack Charlton, who said of him, 'He's got knee problems and hip problems. And everyone knows he's had problems of another kind. We've protected him from the press and from other outsiders, and maybe you could say we've protected him from himself. This is a very special player. I call him a jewel and he is.'

But even legends can't go on forever. After leaving Villa in 1996, he had brief spells at Derby County and Sheffield United before calling it a day two years later at the age of 38. Jack Charlton paid tribute when he said, 'Ireland produced some players over the last 10 or 15 years and, of these, Paul McGrath was the greatest. In his time, he was among the best centre-backs in the world.'

Bryan Robson summed up many people's feelings when he said, 'There were many who felt that Paul's career would end early. The fact that he played at the top level for so long without the benefit of normal training was a tribute to his enormous natural talent.'

By the end of his playing career, Paul had had nine operations on his right knee and three on his left, plus surgery on an Achilles tendon. He also had arthritis behind his right knee. Even Barry Sheen would have been proud of that.

Reflecting on it all, he said later, 'I have made mistakes along the way but I don't have too many regrets. There have been some great times, especially with the Republic. One regret I do have is the fact I didn't behave myself at Manchester United. If I had done myself more favours I probably could have stayed on for longer at Old Trafford. But, having said that, I had a great time at Aston Villa – especially when we won the Coca-Cola Cup when we beat United in the final.

'I was told to retire at 29 and could have taken that option but I would not have sacrificed another eight years playing the game – and two World Cups – for the problems I have now. It would have been more horrendous to have missed all that. I thought I'd be finished at 32 or 33 but I managed to keep on going until I was nearly 38 and I don't regret that, despite the problems I have now.'

Now I love a sherbet and a lot of players' drinking has been greatly exaggerated, but I won't make light of the problems drink caused to Paul McGrath. In spite of his harsh background and massive personal problems, he faced them all – indeed, he wrote a very frank book about them – and became one of the finest players of his generation. A man like that has got to be one of my all-time heroes, hasn't he?

CHAPTER 20

PELE

I guess there is one man you can't leave out of any list of football legends – Pele. He just has to be there. I've never played against him or met him, and I was too young really to watch him in his prime. It doesn't matter a bit.

I'd love to say I'd played against him, who wouldn't? Even in my wildest dreams, I don't think he'd have turned up at Layer Road in Colchester for a friendly. He might have made it to Highbury as he would still only have been in his forties when I joined Arsenal, but it never happened. I can't even say that I watched him in his glory days live on TV. I have memories of the televised 1970 World Cup when I was just five and he was the brightest star in a team of Brazilian all-stars, but he quit the international game soon after that.

If people say there is too much football on television nowadays, it's a shame there was so little when the great man was in his prime. His club career was virtually spent with Santos in Brazil, so he might as well have been playing on the moon for all we knew. Even Brazil's qualifying matches for the World Cup – on the rare occasions they had to qualify – were all South American affairs, so we only saw him on television once every four years when the finals came round. Yet when you ask anyone who has even the faintest interest in football, 'Who is the greatest footballer ever?', there is only one answer: Pele.

I remember my dad Ginge telling me about him and how Pele was only 17 when he played in the 1958 World Cup finals and caused a sensation. He was the youngest player ever to appear in the finals, the youngest goalscorer in World Cup history and the youngest man to pick up a winner's medal. Seventeen is young now, but, back in the 1950s, it was like having a 14- or 15-year-old in your side. 'Youngsters' were 20 or 21, not 17.

I was very young but I remember thinking, Who is this man that Dad keeps going on about? What sticks in my mind is that grainy, almost slow-motion, black-and-white footage of Pele taking a high ball on his chest in the Swedish penalty area in the 1958 final. He controlled it, took it away from the man marking him, flicked it over the head of the defender coming to tackle him and then, as three Swedes closed in, volleyed it past the goalkeeper. As a kid watching those clips, I didn't realise that, even before the kick-off in that 1958 World Cup game, Pele was already a teenager who had made history.

His name is actually Edison Arantes do Nascimento –

he was named after the American inventor Thomas Edison – and his father was a footballer whose career was ended early by a knee injury. His family initially nicknamed him 'Dico' but, so the legend goes, at school he couldn't pronounce the name of his favourite player, Vasco da Gama goalkeeper Bile. It came out Pele, so that's what the other kids called him. As with a lot of nicknames, the poor guy lumbered with it wasn't too keen on it. He thought that Pele was such a rubbish name that he was once suspended from school for two days for punching a kid who kept calling him that. You can guess what happened next – they all called him Pele even more often.

The man himself would have preferred to be called Edson, which is practically his real name. 'Edson sounded so much more serious and important,' he has said. His family still use the name Dico (I wonder if Lee Dixon knows that?) but that wouldn't do for a Brazilian footballer, would it?

He'd been born in poverty – we're talking really poor here – in a shanty town in Bauro, Sao Paulo, and earned extra money by shining shoes on match days at the local football club. The family was so broke they didn't have a proper football to play with, so the young lad practised with a sock full of newspaper or even a grapefruit! But it was obvious, no matter what he played with, the kid had talent. He could have done keepie-uppies with a stick of rhubarb. When he was 15, he joined Sao Paulo's massive Santos FC junior team and after just one season made it to the senior level.

Here the nickname problem came up again – at one stage he was called 'Gasolina'. He says that, as the youngest member of the team, whenever they wanted some coffee brought to them – not difficult in Brazil – he was chosen to fetch it and told, 'Don't spare the gasoline.' Happily, the name didn't stick, which is a bit of good fortune for everyone. Just imagine: 'Ladies and gentlemen, tonight meet the greatest footballer in history – Gasolina!' It sounds like a Brazilian drag queen.

He wasn't fetching the coffee for too long though. He was in the first team at 16 – he scored on his debut – and at 17 was Santos's top scorer. He also made his international debut against Argentina – he scored, of course – and was in the party for the World Cup finals in Sweden, where the rest of the world was about to find out what Brazilians already knew.

He didn't play in the first two games, missing out on a goalless draw against England (the first 0–0 in World Cup finals history), but made it into the starting line-up for the third game, against Russia. He wore the number ten shirt that he, more than anyone else in history, was to make his own. The only surprise was that he didn't score, but he made up for it by getting the only goal of the game in the quarter-final where Brazil beat Wales – yes, I said Wales – to go through to the semi-finals.

There they took on France and won 5–2, with Gasolina scoring a second-half hat-trick in the space of 23 minutes. He was still only 17. Then came that goal against Sweden in the final. The Brazilians even gave the Swedes a goal start by letting them take a fourth-minute lead just to scare the bookies, but they could have given them two or three and it wouldn't have made any difference. To cap it all, Pele even scored with a header in the final minute. He was carried aloft by his team-mates at the end of the game and pictures of him sobbing with joy were wired around the world.

The Brazilians had great players like Didi, Zagallo and Garrincha, but it was Pele who was the star of the show. In the four matches he played in, he'd scored six goals, making him joint runner-up in the goals tally behind an astonishing 13 from France's Just Fontaine. Thirteen goals at a World Cup finals and yet you're not the name on everyone's lips – talk about bad timing!

The great shame is that in Europe we hardly saw him at all before the next World Cup in Chile in 1962. Imagine what it must have been like during those four years seeing him play for Santos every week. He was scoring an average of more than a goal a game and, if you take friendlies into account, in two of those seasons he scored a hundred goals or more. It was phenomenal.

There is some blurred film on the internet which looks as though it was taken in the Victorian era, but you can still sense how far above the other players he was. Brazilians were hardly ever allowed to play abroad in those days until they were coming to the end of their careers, so there was also a strong argument for saying that the Brazilian league was the toughest in the world, packed as it was with their best players. I know they've never been famous for their defending but that makes no difference – he was scoring goals left, right and centre, year after year.

Pele should have been at his peak in the 1962 World Cup but injury forced him out after just two games. In footage of one of them, however, he can be seen steaming through the Chile defence for a stunning solo goal. Four men are beaten by the run: one is left for dead as he puts the ball one side of him and runs the other, and another is simply bulldozed aside by Pele's strength. It's a measure of Brazilian dominance of the 1962 tournament that even without him they won it by a country mile, so he still picked up a winner's medal. Clubs in Spain and Italy wanted to break the bank to bring him over to Europe but he was declared 'a national treasure' and not allowed to leave the country.

England and 1966 should have been the tournament that he dominated above all others, but it wasn't to be either. He scored in the opening game against Bulgaria despite a constant series of brutal tackles. Defenders reckoned he wouldn't be much danger if he was in a hospital bed. That meant he missed the next game, a 3–1 defeat by Hungary and returned, not fully fit, for a must-win match against Portugal.

That game is remembered now for the way he was constantly hacked down by the Portuguese. In the second half, he had to hobble off after two vicious tackles by Joao Morais in the space of a few seconds. He limped back on, heavily bandaged, but he was a passenger for the rest of the match as the Brazilians went out of the competition.

The English referee George McCabe, now dead, was widely criticised for the way he allowed the Portuguese to treat the Brazilians, especially Pele. One observer wrote,

'Pele would say that it was only when he saw the incident on film that he realised how bad it was. He would swear, then, never to play in a World Cup again. The indulgent, flaccid English referee, George McCabe, allowed Morais to stay on the field, so that now Portugal were playing against ten men.'

People often ask how the great players from the past would fare in modern football. Well, I think Pele would be an even greater player today than he was then. The reason is simple: in those days you practically had to kill someone before action was taken against you. Players are much better protected by referees now than they were then.

I think 1966 changed him as a player. He vowed he would never get intimidated or booted off the pitch again and he became a lot more physical himself. Only 5ft 8in tall, he had to protect himself, as it was the law of the jungle. He went back to South America and carried on scoring goals by the lorry load. In 1967, the two sides in the Nigerian civil war even organised a 48-hour ceasefire so they could watch him play in a friendly match in Lagos.

Two years later, he made history again when he scored his 1,000th goal in competitive football. That goal on 19 November 1969 was a penalty – the worst he ever took, he said – against Vasco da Gama in the Maracan Stadium in front of 80,000 fans, not to mention all the TV cameras. Before the kick was taken, Pele and the goalkeeper agreed that Pele should have the ball if he scored and the keeper would have it if he missed. He didn't miss. Talk about a set-up – you couldn't choreograph it better, could you? It was in the biggest football ground in the world and with the media all watching. Bit of luck.

Thousands of fans then invaded the pitch and the game was held up for 30 minutes as the crowd went wild. Most of them were home supporters too. It had taken Pele 909 games to become the first man to reach the 1,000-goal milestone and he was carried around the field on the shoulders of the fans holding the ball aloft. Pele then made a speech appealing for better treatment of Brazil's poor children before the game could be restarted.

After that, how could he top it? Easy really. He decided to play in the Mexico World Cup finals after all. Only after Brazil said pretty please, though. The Brazilian side of 1970 is constantly called 'the greatest team ever'. Apart from Pele, they had players like Carlos Alberto, Jairzinho, Gerson, Tostao and Rivelino in their ranks and, even though the goalkeeper Felix was a bit shaky, it didn't matter, because the other team rarely got that far down the pitch.

England, Romania and Czechoslovakia were all beaten in the first round. Pele didn't score against England – he had to be content with laying on the only goal of the game for Jairzinho – but he did against the other two nations. In the game against the Czechs, he almost scored from ten yards inside his own half, when he saw the keeper off his line in the distance and only missed by a whisper with his long-range shot.

In the semi-final against Uruguay, he came up with my own favourite moment when he raced on to a diagonal ball from Tostao with only the keeper to beat. He left the ball alone to pass one side of the keeper while he ran the other. Then he changed direction and collected it – only to spoil it all by pulling his shot too far back and across the face of the goal. Perhaps he wasn't a natural goalscorer after all!

In the final, Italy were beaten 4–1. Pele opened the scoring with a header when he rose above the massive Italian Facchetti, and in the dying minutes he gently rolled the ball to Carlos Alberto for the fourth goal. It was just great. It's still awesome to watch almost four decades later. So Pele ended up with his third World Cup winner's medal – the only man so far ever to do so.

He played his final game for Santos in 1974 and then finished his career with two seasons at the New York Cosmos. In fact, he only played for those two clubs throughout the three decades he was at the top. Some people might criticise him for ending up playing 'Mickey Mouse' football in the States, but I have no problem with it whatsoever. I'm sure he was the best-paid player in Brazil during his career, but he wouldn't have earned bundles. He'd served his country well and won three World Cups and it was time to go and hunt the filthy dollar.

Pele was still only in his mid-thirties when he then turned out alongside English ex-pros like Charlie Aitken of Aston Villa, Keith Eddy of Watford and Steve Hunt of Aston Villa. He gave football a great boost in the States but it was never going to become the number-one sport there – there's too much competition from their own home-grown games like American football, baseball and basketball.

In October 1977, he played his last game of football in an exhibition match between the Cosmos and Santos. There was a capacity crowd at the Yankee Stadium and before the kick-off he asked them to say the word 'love' three times. Well, it was the 1970s. Pele played the first half for the Cosmos, and – what a turn-up for the books – scored from a free-kick. In the second half, he turned out for Santos. At the end of the match, he ran around the field with an American flag in one hand and a Brazilian one in the other, then he was carried around the field again on the shoulders of the other players. The man must have lost count of the number of times he was carried around a football field in his career.

There's always a bit of an argument when it comes to career statistics for Pele but it's generally accepted that he scored 1,282 goals in 1,363 games between 1956 and 1977, scoring a hat-trick 91 times. And there's more. He hit four goals 31 times, five on six occasions and in one game he hit eight!

If you ask anyone in England to name a famous Brazilian, then they'd all go for Pele – he's even more famous than Ronnie Biggs. (He's associated with Brazil anyway, ain't he?) And there's only one sportsman who can compare with Pele when it comes to what he achieved and world fame and that's Muhammad Ali. Of course, Ali was The Greatest to many, but football is the leading sport in the world, without a shadow of a doubt. It's only in North America where it doesn't rate as the biggest of all sports. That's why Pele is so instantly recognised and admired. Plus, of course, his is a great rags-to-riches story.

It didn't all end there, though. He's probably just as famous today as he was at the height of his career. In 1992, he was appointed a United Nations ambassador for ecology and the environment, and later he became Brazil's 'Extraordinary Minister for Sport'. In 1997, even the Queen gave him an honorary British knighthood.

Pele might not have made the astonishing sums that present-day players earn, but he has become a wealthy man over the years with a variety of sponsorship and business deals. It was recently calculated that he earns around £14 million a year from various endorsement deals ranging from Coca-Cola to MasterCard. The Brazilian oil giant Petrobras paid him to boost its global image with investors, and Coke pays for a mobile Pele museum that travels his home country, featuring his exploits on the pitch. Electronics firm Samsung hired him to act as an ambassador throughout Southeast Asia and he was paid to walk around with a Nokia mobile phone whenever he was in Brazil. He is constantly booked for corporate functions and has admitted, 'No doubt I am earning more money with my endorsements than I ever earned playing soccer. But I don't think I'm a very good businessman. I act too much with my heart. I have a big responsibility. So many people trust me.' That's why he doesn't advertise tobacco and alcohol firms.

He also made headlines when he boosted a different kind of 'keepie-uppie' campaign – for Viagra. It's not as though he's been lacking in firepower himself: he's had two wives and six children at the last count. 'I think it is stronger to do an ad when you do not have the problem and are wanting to help, rather than when you do have the problem,' was his explanation. 'When you have the problem, of course you will want to help everyone else with the same problem.'

So granddad Pele has no problem with lead in his pencil and wants to make sure no other guys have either. I'll go along with that.

And what makes him an even bigger hero to me is that he's all in favour of players having sex before matches too. 'Having sex is not the problem,' he says. 'It's what comes with it that the coaches are against. Sometimes, the players stay up late and don't sleep well. And that's where the problem lies. They must be ready to play.

'Footballers are humans and there are pressures on them too. People expect them to play their best all the time. When they can't, it leads to stress. The stress can affect their sex lives. This happens with Brazilian footballers too.'

Why should he be embarrassed to talk about things like that? I don't think he gives a shit, especially as he says his own sex life is 'normal'. Goals, beautiful women, kids and Viagra. What a man. And he says he hasn't minded being called Pele for years now – he's used to it. Well, that helps doesn't it?